AF568067

KNOWLEDGE SOCIETY

Knowledge Society

Oppurtunities and Challenges

Edited by

P V L Raju

2010

Icfai Books
The Icfai University Press

KNOWLEDGE SOCIETY: OPPORTUNITIES AND CHALLENGES

Editors: P V L Raju

First Edition: 2010
Printed in India

Published by

The Icfai University Press
52, Nagarjuna Hills, Punjagutta
Hyderabad, India – 500 082
Phone: (+91) (040) 23430–368, 369, 370, 372, 373, 374
Fax: (+91) (040) 23352521, 23435386
E-mail: info@icfaibooks.com, icfaibooks@icfai.org, ssd@icfai.org

ISBN: 9788131401392

Editorial Team: V Chaitanya and K Prabhakar

CONTENTS

Overview

The emergence of knowledge economy is one of the most dramatic shifts to have taken place in modern society since the Industrial Revolution of the 19th century. In traditional economy, the added value occurs through interactive potential of financial capital, men and material. However, in the knowledge economy, the added value is gained through the application of knowledge to work processes, products and services. In other words, the performance differential is attributable to the intellectual resources rather than the physical resources. Traditional resources of production are less important than knowledge-based economy. Knowledge has shifted from its ivory tower existence and is generated contextually for products and services that have commercial implication.

With knowledge as the main organizational currency, firms must be able to learn fast, and adapt to the new challenges. They also need to ensure that the workforce develops and shares strategic valuable-knowledge and continuously improves and innovates in products and services. Peter Drucker says that the next society that is already emerging will be a knowledge society. He has also coined the popular term 'knowledge worker.' Essentially, knowledge workers are those whose jobs require knowledge-intensive skills. In the changed scenario of workforce, HR practices will play a significant role in shaping, influencing and enhancing the capability of knowledge workers. The focus has to shift from controlling people to a strategy to gain employee commitment on a voluntary basis. Knowledge will become the key resource and knowledge workers will be the critical group in the workforce. Drucker argues that the three main characteristics of a knowledge worker are borderlessness, upward mobility and the potential for failure as well as success. Altogether, these characteristics make knowledge society a tough, competitive one, both for individuals and organizations.

Knowledge management as a managerial concept demands a change in thinking on strategy, structure, and resources and should be accompanied by commitment of resources in terms of time, effort and money. The biggest managerial challenge is tapping the tacit knowledge hidden in the people. It is relatively easy to harness explicit knowledge that is embedded in policies, procedures and organizational routines through IT and other knowledge management mechanisms. But tapping the tacit knowledge poses a great challenge to an organization.

HR assumes special significance in the context of present-day economy. HR practitioners ought to be the thought-leaders for the people side of the enterprise and facilitate employers' and workers' dialogue process to meet the future challenges. Human resources are the key differentiators for the effectiveness of knowledge management. It is the people who create knowledge and are the repositories of such knowledge. The leadership and the style of managing people create the enabling culture. Ultimately, this defines the effectiveness of knowledge management. Thus, there is an urgent need to align HR policies with the distinctive traits of knowledge workers. Equally, there is an urgent need to link HR management to knowledge management in order to enhance organizational effectiveness.

The book has three sections: Challenges of HR; KM Issues; and Cases.

Section I: Challenges of HR

The first article, "**Managing Knowledge Work: HR Perspectives**", is by *P V L Raju*. In the knowledge society, deployment of knowledge that serves as an agent for the betterment of the firm is an effective competitive advantage. Knowledge has shifted from its ivory tower existence and is generated contextually for products and services that have commercial implications. HRM has to make a radical shift in the management of people. A firm with a higher level of employee commitment contributes significantly to organizational effectiveness.

The second article, "**Knowledge Management and Role of HR**", is by *G R K Murty*. With the advent of knowledge society, there is a shift of business towards 'knowledge economy.' This has brought knowledge to the forefront and knowledge management has become an important strategy for organizations. Once knowledge is transformed from an activity status to an object status, it becomes information power. Knowledge management activities are a mix of knowledge and information. KM essentially aims at value addition to the users.

The third article, "**Employee Commitment: Bridging HRM with KM**", is by *Tapan K Panda, Tapas K Panda* and *Subrat K Mishra*. Employee commitment depends on the sense of belongingness of the employee towards the organization. The article focuses on the element of trust that will help organizations to foster and share knowledge amongst employees. The model of Psychological Contract by Guest and Conway (1997) is discussed in the article. It also analyses the factors that mediate the relationship between HRM and KM.

The fourth article, "**Emerging Global Issues in Human Resource Management**", is written by *William J Rothwell* and *Tiffani D Payne*. Employment in knowledge society poses unique challenges to HR such as launching and sustaining effective performance management system, building and maintaining effective recruitment system and aligning revised management initiatives with individual preferences. Key challenges in recruitment are building and sustaining effective recruitment efforts both in good and bad economic times and keeping pace with e-recruitment issues. The role of training is building organizational talent. Training should move away from teaching to learning. By learning, individuals are empowered to do things themselves. Rewarding human performance is really very complex rather than merely rewarding pay for performance. The real challenge is to provide elegant but simple incentive systems that promise dependable rewards for specific results that matter to individuals. HR practitioners must become true leaders for the people side of the enterprise to help employers and workers meet the present and future challenges.

The fifth article, "**Challenges for HR Professionals in the Knowledge-Driven Era**", is authored by *Rajashree Vyas*. The affairs of a business world such as rapid growth of innovation, changing legislations, growing lawsuits, etc., are evolving at a faster pace in today's world. Universal access to HR-related information and self-service options will be allowed by the new technology that is part of globalization process. The practice of human resource management is expected to contribute to global networking. The future of HR is shifting from support function to more of a strategic partnership which helps the organization achieve its objective.

Section II: KM Issues

The first article of this section, "**Harnessing Tacit Knowledge in Organizations**", is written by *Daniel Ashish* and *S Senthil Kumar*. Harnessing tacit knowledge calls for suitable HR interventions in organizations. Incentives that can be used by organizations to encourage knowledge sharing must include rewards, creating appropriate conditions and infrastructure. Knowledge map plays an important role in facilitating the right knowledge being transferred to the right person. But building such maps requires an organized effort throughout the organization.

Any successful initiative to harness tacit knowledge needs to break psychological barriers rather than organizational barriers.

The next article, "**Recruiting Knowledge Workers**", is by *Karen Unwin.* Recruitment and OD strategy go hand in hand. The relationship between recruitment, business strategy and organizational culture is so intertwined that the recruiter must adopt a holistic approach rather than treat them as different components. Business success depends on attracting and retaining talented specialists and containing frequent turnover of employees as knowledge will also leave along with the employees. As Drucker says, knowledge workers don't believe they are paid to work 9 to 5; they believe they are paid to be effective.

The third article, "**Retaining Talent in Knowledge Economy**", is by *Gurdeep S Hora.* HR professionals are responding through deliberate and conscious people management strategies in the present knowledge economy. Recruitment is no longer a one-time exercise. The companies have to constantly monitor performance and scan the environment for optimal organizational performance. In a highly competitive knowledge society, performance of the organizations is critically linked to the quality and the performance of its human resources. Companies focus on systematically communicating and keeping in touch with the employees. They encourage innovation and ingenuity that provide opportunities to employees to upgrade their skills.

The fourth article of this section, "**Managing Career in Knowledge Society**", is authored by *Radha Mohan Chebolu.* The growing 'career consciousness' among the youth to pursue a career-building strategy, while working in the organization, is found to be the reality today. Employees often interpret tangible signs of progress in the workplace as signals that they are on the right path of progress in their career. The necessity for toning up the abilities and skills required to stay fit in the competition are increasingly realized by the young generation. The concept of job security gets redefined in the light of changing paradigms of economy driven by global competition. For achieving uniformity and synthesis in idea implementation, people need to be trained on multidisciplinary lines with a strong zeal for efficiency and merit.

The next article, **"Virtual Teams in the Knowledge Society"**, is by *Sumati Reddy* of the ICFAI University. The knowledge society has brought one major development where individuals can participate in different kinds of work, without actually relocating to the place of work. Management of virtual teams requires paying greater attention to the criterion of team formation, so that each member contributes to the overall effectiveness of the team. It is important to make efforts to build rapport and relationship among team members as this will determine the team's communication and performance.

The sixth article, **"Training and Development in Knowledge Society"**, is by *K Mallikarjunan.* Training programs in a knowledge society dominated by IT should be directed towards the fullest exploitation of opportunities that are facilitated by ceaseless progress of technology. The knowledge economy calls for thoughtful strategies to update the skills of the personnel. The most distinguishing feature of a knowledge society is its ability to collect, cull and interpret information through properly trained employees. Knowledge management is the framework for synergizing the processes of knowledge production, sharing and application for maximum effectiveness and efficiency.

The seventh and last article in this section is titled as **"Knowledge Management: Why Learning from the past is not Enough!"** and is authored by *Rogério dePaula* and *Gerhard Fischer.* Traditional knowledge management approaches aim to archive information from the past, which implies that the information needs of the future are expected to be the same as they were in the past. Knowledge is presented as a commodity to be acquired, never as a human struggle to understand, to overcome falsity and to stumble upon the truth.

The design perspective for KM goes beyond our reach to allow reciprocity. It recognizes the key role of human agency in knowledgeable performances. Changes will take place only if those involved in the design and development of innovations come to appreciate the delicate balance between existing cultural practices and innovations.

Section III: Cases

The first case study, "**Knowledge Management at Tata Steel**", is by *Ajay Kumar* and *Sanjib Dutta* of the ICFAI University. Tata Steel started with a small group of people from within the organization. In 2001, Tata Steel developed a 'KM index' to evaluate the performance of individual employees in the KM initiative. Later, it linked performance evaluation to KM and used a balanced scorecard to monitor the performance of individual employees, divisions, as well as the organization as a whole. Later in early 2003, Tata Steel was recognized as one of Asia's Most Admired Knowledge Enterprises (MAKE).

The second case, "**KM Initiatives in India: Key Success Drivers**", is written by *Swati Raman.* The research article focuses on the various dimensions of KM and does a literature survey. Also, it provides a pragmatic view of KM initiatives in the Wipro and Infosys.

The third case study "**From Community of Practice to On Demand Workplace: IBM's Journey in Knowledge Management**" is written by *Jayaprada, Minita Sinha* and *T R Venkatesh.* IBM began its journey in KM in 1994 with the design of the ICM (Intellectual Capital Management) AssetWeb framework, which supported community of practice. Research at IBM Global Service led to the design and development of Lotus Discovery System which was later withdrawn. In 2003, On Demand Workplace was installed in IBM, where employees could share and transfer knowledge across the globe. IBM reflected on how On Demand Workplace would fare in the market and whether it would be accepted by different organizations.

Section I

Challenges of HR

1

Managing Knowledge Work: HR Perspectives

P V L Raju

The elementary requirement for any business firm is the creation and deployment of knowledge, which serves as an agent for the betterment of the firm. Moreover, the deviations among two or more firms can be analyzed based on the level of knowledge and their respective abilities in harnessing the knowledge. In this context there lies an implicit need for aligning HR policies to knowledge management.

Managing knowledge and knowledge workers is undoubtedly the most challenging job for an organization in the knowledge society. In the current knowledge era, knowledge management (KM) is considered to be the panacea to address the problems of business competitiveness. The context for managing knowledge is provided by the following factors:

- Information age demands restructuring of work.
- Wealth-creation has shifted to knowledge-based activities.
- Growing importance of knowledge work and knowledge workers.

Knowledge is a fluid of framed experience, values, contextual information and expert insight that provides a framework for evaluating and incorporating new experiences

Source: HRM Review, October 2005.

and information. The primary objective of a business enterprise is creation and deployment of knowledge that contributes to its productivity. The performance differences among firms result from their different stock of knowledge and their differing abilities in fostering and harnessing the knowledge. For a broad understanding, knowledge is bifurcated into two: explicit and tacit knowledge. The former is information that is codified and can be transferred from one individual to another through a formal communication system. Tacit knowledge, on the other hand, cannot be communicated in a formal communication channel, and according to an individual's 'mental model' and is not easily transferable.

The relationship between knowledge and wealth creation is as old as the mountains. The importance of managing knowledge has long since been recognized. F W Taylor, considered as the father of scientific management principles, explored how to manage knowledge of work process. His famous "Time and Motion" theory deals with the knowledge required to carry out work tasks residing in the knowledge management process. During the process of determining the most efficient way to conduct the work process, Taylor was attempting to manage the knowledge in the work process. Henry Ford's mass production system is a classic example of application of the principles of scientific management to work practices. In the traditional method, before the dawn of knowledge era, knowledge was more academic and cognitive in nature. In contrast, knowledge in the context of knowledge economy is application-oriented and is relevant in the shop floor context. This implies that knowledge has shifted from its ivory tower existence and is generated contextually for products and services that have commercial implication.

From the perspective of human resources, it is imperative to understand the distinctive traits of knowledge work and knowledge workers. Generally, knowledge workers expect considerable latitude in their work environment. This is a natural corollary of the nature of work that is characterized by creativity and problem solving. The skill sets are complex and demand greater autonomy. The knowledge workers themselves are the most appropriate people to decide how to initiate, plan and coordinate their major tasks. The second distinguishing factor is that there is a need to work remote from the employing firm, typically located at the client's premises. This physical collocation is an important management issue for the employer. For example, client company may be inclined to offer employment to knowledge workers who are good performers and prove to be less expensive if employed directly. HR has to play a proactive role and should focus on the strategies to aid retention. Of late, the term "gold collar" worker (Kelley 1990) is applied to knowledge workers. It essentially means that these workers need to be managed carefully and should be provided with very congenial work environment and fairly generous employment terms.

HR practices play a significant role in shaping, influencing and enhancing the capability of knowledge workers. The selection, appraisal and reward system of knowledge workers has to be differently oriented keeping in view the above factors. If employees do not possess or develop the right competencies and if they are not motivated to create and share knowledge, the organizations will not be able to exploit its knowledge base effectively.

HRM has to make radical shift in the management of people. It has to shift its emphasis from controlling people and consciously pursue a strategy to gain their commitment on a voluntary basis. Robert Lavering in his book *A Great Place to Work* observes, a firm with higher levels of employee commitment is a better place to work than with lower levels—employees help each other more; they are happier, more excited to come to work, more collaborative and friendlier. There is an urgent need to align HR policies with the distinctive traits of knowledge workers. There is also an equal need to link HRM to Knowledge Management in order to enhance organizational performance.

(P V L Raju is faculty member of ICFAI National College, Hyderabad and consulting editor for HRM Review. He can be reached at rajupvl@icfaipress.org).

2

Knowledge Management and Role of HR

G R K Murty

In the recent past, work has shifted from "hands to mind." Peter Drucker once said that organizations of the future would be knowledge-based and would essentially employ specialists who direct and discipline their own performance through organized feedback from colleagues, customers and corporate headquarters. Knowledge management, as a concept with people at the center-stage has, thus, emerged as a new management tool in the corporate world, which this article proposes to discuss.

In the recent past, knowledge and knowledge management have generated a lot of interest among corporate leaders. It is, of course, the advent of information society and its move towards "knowledge economy" that has brought knowledge and the importance of its management within organizations to the forefront. But this doesn't mean that there was no knowledge earlier and that people were not concerned about its management. Knowledge has been with us since mankind came into existence. Indeed, it is the accumulation and application of knowledge over centuries that transformed the agrarian society into industrial society and ultimately into information society. The only difference from the past is that

Source: HRM Review, November, 2004.

today knowledge has become one of the key factors of production. In fact, many are now considering knowledge as the only economic resource in the knowledge society. The very fact that we consider today's economy to be knowledge economy places "knowledge" at the center-stage. Against this background, this article attempts to define what is knowledge, and what for and how knowledge management is accomplished, and the key role of human resources in effective knowledge management.

Knowledge and Its Varied Facets

Knowledge creation is a process of value addition to the existing knowledge through innovation. It means the more of it we have, the more we are likely to generate and that is what we have been witnessing all along. Simply put, knowledge creates knowledge and in the process it bestows competitive advantage on its owners leading to wealth creation. According to Davenport and Prusak, "Knowledge is a fluid mix of framed experience, values, contextual information, and expert insight that provides a framework for evaluating and incorporating new experiences and information. It originates and is applied in the minds of knower. In organizations, it often becomes embedded not only in documents or repositories but also in organizational routines, processes, practices, and norms."[1]

In the context of knowledge management in organizations, knowledge does not necessarily mean what is there in journals and books, for that is only information. It is only what is read, manipulated, communicated and embedded in people's mind that becomes knowledge. That is the precise reason why knowledge in the form of skills cannot be codified, captured, and managed, but can be acquired only through interaction with people who have such skills. It is only that knowledge, which can be captured, processed, and managed through IT. There are thus two approaches to manage knowledge in organizations: First, "People track" and second, "IT track." The People-track approach focuses on the management of people, i.e., assessing, changing, and improving individual skills of people and their behavior, while IT-track focuses on management of explicit knowledge or information.

Tacit knowledge is mostly supposed to exist only in the human minds. It is considered as a by-product of interaction of people among themselves and with the environment. It remains in the unconscious and we may not even be aware of its existence. To put it otherwise, "we can know more of it than being able to talk about it." On the other hand, "know-how" is knowledge created out of practice and collectively shared by a group. Such implicit knowledge can be captured and codified as information for future use. For instance, a computer servicing company can list probable failures that can be anticipated based on past experiences and also record plausible remedies for all such problems and make it available for servicing workforce as an operating guide. Similarly, a five-star hotel can document the ingredients and process involved in making a Chinese dish and make it available for a new chef to master its preparation through a few trials. "Know-how" that resulted from the conversion of tacit knowledge into explicit knowledge can be transferred to others through a well-structured learning process.

Why and How of Knowledge Management

Knowledge management is basically concerned with explicit knowledge, know-how or implicit knowledge and tacit knowledge. These three are quite interrelated and, in fact, cannot be segmented, as knowledge management is an outcome of people's interaction with other people, data and information and the environment in which they function. We should, therefore, treat knowledge as an activity and not as an object. Once knowledge is transformed from an activity status to an object status, it becomes a piece of information, and then it becomes pretty easy to manage it through information management systems. That is where technology comes handy in effectively managing knowledge. Technology facilitates quick transmission and exchange of information by cataloguing the knowledge created by the organizational members and makes it accessible to the right people, paving way for enhanced knowledge sharing.

Most of the knowledge management activities undertaken by organizations are found to be a mix of knowledge and information management. Knowledge management essentially aims at value addition to users. It leads not only to improvement and innovations in the existing operations, but also adds value to the existing pool of organizational knowledge by filtering, synthesizing and interpreting knowledge by making use of the feedback from the users. Unless it goes beyond mere search and acquisition of knowledge, it cannot play a significant role in achieving organizational efficiency. In this context, it is "collaborative technologies" rather than the information management tools that are found to be more competent to handle knowledge management.

In a globalized economy, companies face stiff competition as consumers are enjoying an unprecedented array of choices for goods and services across the globe. It is the agile responsiveness with which businesses can deliver services to customers who have become the key determinants of survival. It is often found that intelligence-gathering and market intelligence have enabled many Japanese companies to succeed. That is how knowledge management has taken center-stage in collecting bits and pieces of information relating to customers and competition in the market and synthesizing it into ready-to-use information to face competition.

There is yet another fear among the organizations: A lot of tacit knowledge that exists only in the minds of people often found walking away from the organizations as people left them for one reason or another. Similarly, "downsizing" resorted to by companies as a cost-reduction exercise has also resulted in "knowledge scarcity." It is to capture and retain such a critical knowledge within the organization that knowledge management has become a must. The importance of knowledge management in organizations has been well-captured by Stewart in his statement: "Knowledge has become the primary ingredient of what we make, do, buy and sell. As a result, managing it—finding and growing intellectual capital, storing it, selling it, sharing it—has become the most important economic task of individuals, business and nations."[2]

Driven by this philosophy, organizations—small and big—are today striving to build knowledge management structure on the following lines:

- Define what is 'K' and what it is not for the organization.
- Locate the centers of the organization where such 'K' is generated.
- Convert data and information into 'K'.
- Suck it out from people who give birth to it and transfer it into a depository.
- Organize the depository and make it freely accessible to everyone.
- Make the depository "intelligent" so that it constantly renews itself.

Role of HR in Knowledge Management

We have seen that knowledge management essentially deals with acquisition, construction and transfer or sharing of knowledge among the members of the organization so as to facilitate better accomplishment of organizational goals. Research findings also indicate that the organizational culture and the communication strategy that promotes free dialog among the team members are the two critical factors for effective knowledge sharing. The very fact that knowledge is collated from and, in turn, shared among the members of an organization and the culture of an organization that facilitates smooth sharing of knowledge, highlights the criticality of human resources in the management of knowledge.

Learning in the organizations mostly occurs within groups. Social learning may be defined as the process by which knowledge and practices built in the system are transmitted across different work situations and across time and the procedures that facilitate generative learning, which enables an organization to react creatively to sudden and unanticipated developments. Research findings indicate that effective social learning in the organizations calls for empowerment of staff to seek and experiment with new knowledge; trust and mutual respect among the members; a culture that encourages employees to take risks; "forgiving culture" of mistakes that encourages knowledge construction based on the lessons learnt; cohesion among the team members that encourages sharing of knowledge and goals; and transparent decision-making across the organization. The scope for social learning is found to be enhanced with the use of "dialog" which involves going beyond individual consciousness into mutual communing to perceive reality correctly and to the learning of a larger reality. The value of dialog in knowledge development can be appreciated from the fact that it facilitates interpretation of new meanings through collaborative thinking and mutual communing. All this only highlights the importance of human resources in the entire gamut of knowledge management.

What Human Resource Management Division (HRMD) Should do for a Better Knowledge Management?

Research findings indicate that HRMD must strive to create essential social learning enablers in an organization to ensure effective knowledge management. Some such critical enablers are:

- Positive communication climate—having a workplace where people can freely approach the manager and say, "Hi! I don't understand this. It might be stupid, but would you please help me figure it out?"
- Effective leadership—workplace that depicts accessibility to their staff, non-judgmental approach to the staff and the issues that they bring to the manager.
- Goal alignment—ensuring cohesiveness between the leaders and team and within the team members enabling everyone to know where the other is heading, listening to everyone's problems and making everyone understand what and why changes are happening.
- Constructive performance management—setting realistic goals before every member and rightly measuring and recording the performance.
- Valuing skills and reward and recognition strategies—the very fact of being valued makes an individual willing to engage in a dialog with teammates, learn and share knowledge with others resulting in team cohesiveness; in short, it is simply practicing the common axiom "praise is better than money."
- Enabling workplace design—having a workplace design that fosters physical proximity, ensures better communication among team members resulting in good engagement in dialog.
- Team-based morale—learning in the organizations is basically a social process of interaction, which is facilitated by dialog, and unless high morale prevails among the team members, dialog cannot take place freely.
- Socializing—feeling good about the colleagues in the team is a great motivating factor to generate a sense of belonging to the group; such identity results in awareness about the expertise possessed by team members; healthy social relations build trust, make people learn faster and make them more creative and productive; and informal socialization leads to better and easy sharing of knowledge.
- Timely induction programs—induction programs conducted for new recruits well in time provide "foundation knowledge" to the raw members;

such programs minimize the scope for misunderstandings and pave way for better working relationships by reducing anxiety and improve the efficiency of new members by letting them know as to what is expected of them.

These enablers are likely to develop a suitable architecture for effective management of knowledge in the organizations, but if not effectively used, they also have the potential to pose challenges to knowledge management.

Conclusion

To be is to learn; to learn is to know and to know is to win. Today, by offering wide range of choices to consumers across the globe at the mere click of a mouse, the Internet world has made consumers a highly knowledgeable lot. To survive in such a competitive world, organizations have to necessarily build knowledge, replenish it, and disseminate it among the members of the organization, so that the accumulated knowledge can be put to use for accomplishing organizational goals. In building up knowledge bases, organizations must be conscious of what is and is not knowledge for the organization and only collate, interpret, synthesize and distribute such knowledge among its members which has a bearing on its performance. It is worth bearing in mind here that IT is only an enabler of knowledge management. Human resources are the keydeciders of the effectiveness of knowledge management for it is they who are instrumental in generating knowledge, learning from new knowledge and using it for the good of the organization. It is the leadership and its style of managing the human resources and the enabling culture that they create in the organizations which ultimately defines the effectiveness of knowledge management.

(G R K Murty is Associate Dean, Academic Wing, The ICFAI University.)

Endnotes

1 Devanport, TH and Prusak, L (1998). "Working Knowledge: How organizations manage what they know. Boston", MA: Harvard Business School Press.

2 Stewart, T A (1997). Intellectual Capital, London. Nicholas Brealey Publishing.

3

Employee Commitment: Bridging HRM with KM

Tapan K Panda, Tapas K Panda and Subrat K Mishra

Most of the work in the knowledge management area explains how technology and systems can create environments for sharing, storing and management of knowledge. However, knowledge management largely depends on the willingness of the employees to share in the organizational context. The willingness to share knowledge depends on the commitment of the employees towards the organization. Employee commitment depends on the sense of belongingness of the employees towards the organization. This paper attempts to build a bridge called trust that will help organizations to have a better climate of industrial relations and a sense of ownership. This will lead towards the development of a knowledge-sharing attitude among the employees.

Sources of competitive advantages are changing over a period of time. Sources like cost advantage, process and market control and proximity to strategic resource boundary are fast losing their strategic sustainability as a source of competitive advantage. Knowledge in both the forms—tacit and explicit—is fast emerging as a critical source of competitive advantage. All along, corporations

Source: The article was published as "Employee Commitment: The Bridge Between Human Resource Management and Knowledge Management" in HRM Review, October, 2005.

have neglected the creation, dissemination and application of knowledge in solving organizational problems and building strategies to exploit business opportunities.

Success of knowledge management (KM) largely depends on retention and growth in quality human resource in organizations. Hence, better human resource management practices, by which the employees will be ready to share their knowledge across the enterprise, are the fundamentals to the success of KM. One can fairly use human resource management tools and concepts to improve the level of willingness of the employees, to share this knowledge and motivate them to contribute through enhanced organizational commitment. KM and transfer are not purely confined to the benefits of learning curve; rather, they extend to strategic contributions in the form of improving environmental hygiene and building better business processes. This paper aims at developing an intermediary variable called organizational commitment, which will augment the KM and transfer across organizations and cultures.

Most of the earlier literature on KM is technology-focused, where organizations can set up structures and systems for enhanced organizational effectiveness (Beaumont and Hunter, 2002; Scarbrough *et al.*, 1993, Ruggles, 1998). Social and human orientation to the strategic KM is of recent origin. Available KM literature has not fully utilized the people management orientation, but has acknowledged that it is necessary to give a perspective of man management in managing knowledge (Storey and Quintas, 2001, Scarbough and Carter, 2000).

Employees' attitude and behavior within the workplace is closely linked with their level of commitment to the organization. Starting from the human relation school of Elton Mayo to the current neo-classical and process schools, theorists have accepted this golden truth. Subsequent research (Chen Francesco, 2000, Iversion and Buttigieg, 1999) has identified that the level of commitment influences the turnover intentions and attrition rates. But the influence of commitment in KM and sharing has not been established. People with high level of commitments and loyalty to enterprises are found to be cocoons on self-isolation and selfish pursuit for career and material gains.

It is worth investigating the link between the level of commitment, workers' feelings towards the organization, and their overall attitude and behavior towards the KM initiatives in the organization. Success of any KM initiative largely depends on the level of motivation of people and their subsequent active role in the KM process (Robertson and O'Malley Hammersley, 2000). Most of the knowledge in the organization is tacit in nature; though some people do not agree with the dichotomous classification of knowledge as either tacit or explicit. Tacit knowledge, either embrained or embodied, is possessed by people (Blacker, 1995) and is often found difficult to codify into explicit form. Knowledge is a resource occurred in human mind (Kim and Mauborgne, 1998). So the personal nature of the tacit knowledge requires willingness on the part of the workers to share and communicate with others (Empson, 2001, William *et al.,* 2001, Kim and Mauborgne, 1998, Morx, 2001).

Ownership of Knowledge in the Organization

There is also an argument and corresponding tension in the organization about the ownership and control of this tacit knowledge, which influences the willingness to share it by the employees. Research (Storey and Barnett, 2000) suggests that knowledge is a resource with a significant amount of potential status and power. It also argues that any attempt to manage, control or codify organizational knowledge is likely to produce internal conflict. The third aspect of evaluating relevance of HRM in KM initiatives is the study of the extent to which involvement of the worker with the organization will lead towards knowledge-sharing. Enterprises with high employee turnover bear the risk of losing the key manpower with specialized knowledge. Therefore, retention of resourceful manpower is the key to effective KM initiative. The personal nature of the knowledge makes us assume that the person should notice the significance of shared knowledge across the organization. This becomes imperative to retain quality manpower with desired knowledge levels. As discussed, there exist conflicting interests between the people who possess the knowledge and the organization which employs them, grooms them and wants them to share the knowledge. This does not make the case of KM initiative an easier and straightforward option for employees to share their tacit knowledge.

The above discussion leads us to identify the genuine factors that make people either share or hoard their knowledge and also the motivations which make them to continue on the roll for the same organization. We will also focus on the attitude of the employees towards knowledge sharing and the KM *per se* than a mere identification of what motivates them to continue in the same organization. Various human resource practices like recruitment, training and development, job design, welfare programs, level of autonomy involved, exercise of a culture of openness and mutual trust help in building an environment that will make people to share their tacit knowledge. Higher level of commitment is also reflected on the higher retention rate, better industrial relations and enhanced productivity.

Fairness in decision-making and business practices also influences the level of commitment. When the human resource practices and welfare measures satisfy employee expectations, the employee realizes that his experience and expertise are part of appraisal and reward systems. Then his motivation to share knowledge increases. The earlier concept of role conflict is also a determinant in the level of knowledge-sharing. If the employee finds that sharing and codifying his knowledge will not dilute his status and value of experience, he will be more willing to share the tacit knowledge. At a macro level, organization culture will also decide the level of sharing/hoarding of knowledge among workers. The role relationships and level of effective interaction during the knowledge sharing sessions will also influence the overall attitude of the people towards KM initiatives.

The Role of Commitment Construct

Commitment is associated with other constructs like trust, psychological contract and job satisfaction. Guest and Conway (1947) developed a model of psychological contract. Hislop (2003) modified this model to establish a relationship between commitment and knowledge-sharing attitude. This model explains how the level of commitment affects a wide range of attitude towards the organization and behavior in the workplace. Guest and Conway's model attempts to integrate constructs like commitment, psychological contract and job satisfaction.

Psychological contract represents the perceptions of both the employee and the organization that bring to the employment relationship their internal obligations (Cherriot *et al.,* 1997). This model explains how employees feel about the extent to which the enterprise met their expectations with underlying causes of the feeling and their likely attitudinal and behavioral consequences. (Hislop 2003). In this model, the heart of the psychological contract relates to fairness,

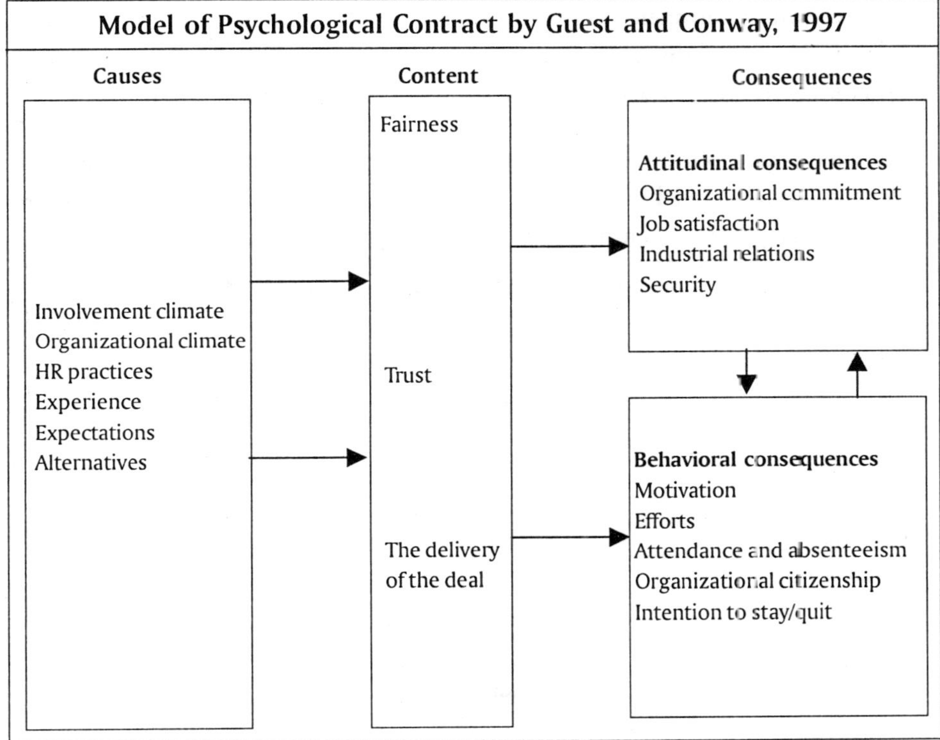

trust and the 'delivery of the deal'. Fairness results from the facts like prevalent sense of equity in the organization, the extent to which people are valued and rewarded for their contribution (Flood *et al.*, 2001). Trust relates to the confidence in someone or something and involves an expectation about future outcomes. Finally, the 'delivery of the deal' relates to the extent to which workers believe that the key promises and obligations they expect of the organization have been met (Guest 1998).

Commitment to an organization is an attitudinal consequence of the psychological contract. A positive psychological contract means that a positive/higher level of commitment has its bearing on the behavioral consequences. However, this model is not free from structural problems. This model does not differentiate between the forms of commitment, viz., affective, continuance and normative. On the external contractual situations, workers can be committed to more than one organization that includes the placement agency, the organization itself, trade unions, working groups, etc. Though there is a set of questions on the very process and commitments of this model, we can summarize this to a fair approximation in explaining the organizational commitment and behavioral consequences.

Now let us take our attention to how knowledge-sharing attitude and behavior of workers are affected by their level of commitment. If the organizations can develop a high level of commitment from workers, then this can have positive

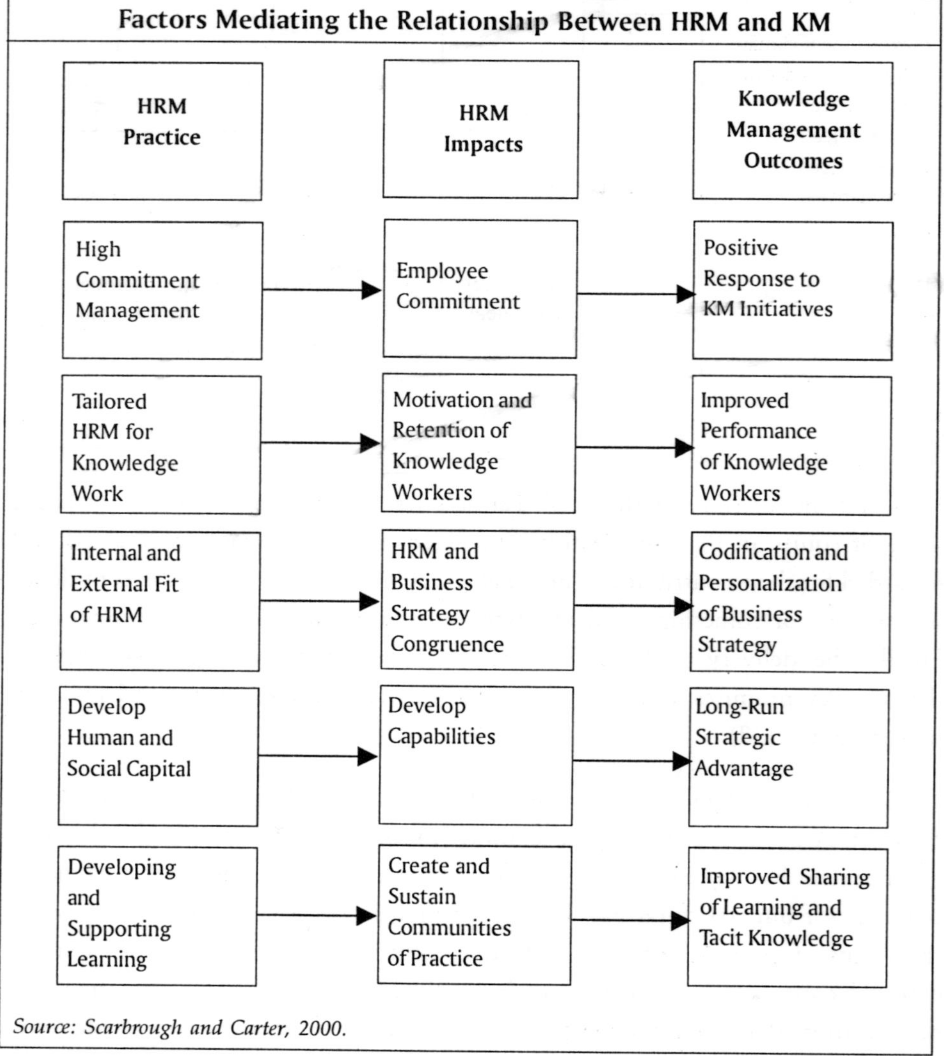

Source: Scarbrough and Carter, 2000.

benefits in the form of increased loyalty, reduced turnover and motivation of workers to provide discretionary effort for the organization (Gallie *et al.*, 2001, Shepherd and Mathews, 2000). Development of trust, commitment and motivation for workers represents one of the key issues in relation to management of knowledge workers. Workers with high level of organizational commitment are less likely to leave, are more likely to be highly motivated and will be more willing to provide extra discretionary effort and be generally willing to share their knowledge within the organization (Storey and Quintas, 2001).

There are five perspectives, which can be used to link HRM with KM (Scarbrough and Carter, 2000). The perspective of 'best practice' facilitates knowledge-sharing and these practices can be used for any organization. The outcomes will be in the form of positive response to the KM initiatives, improved performance of knowledge workers, codification and personalization of business strategy, long-run strategic advantage and improved sharing of learning and tacit knowledge.

Development, use and retention of knowledge capital in organizations (Robertson, O'Malley, Hammersley, 2000) are to some extent dependent upon workers possessing some level of commitment to the organization in which they were working.

Organizational Commitment: An Intervening Variable

Organizational commitment can be linked with knowledge-sharing attitude and behavior (Hislop, 2003). It will affect attitude of workers towards knowledge-sharing activities; extent to which workers actively participate in KM and knowledge sharing; loyalty of workers to their organization and the likelihood that they will remain with them. He modified Conway's Model to link knowledge-sharing with organizational commitment.

Conclusion and Future Research Issues

However, a conceptual formulation like this is based on an assumption that attitudes affect behavior. So when one can influence the attitude of employees through HRM initiatives, it will influence the behavior towards KM. It is necessary to explain the relationship between organizational commitment, attitude towards

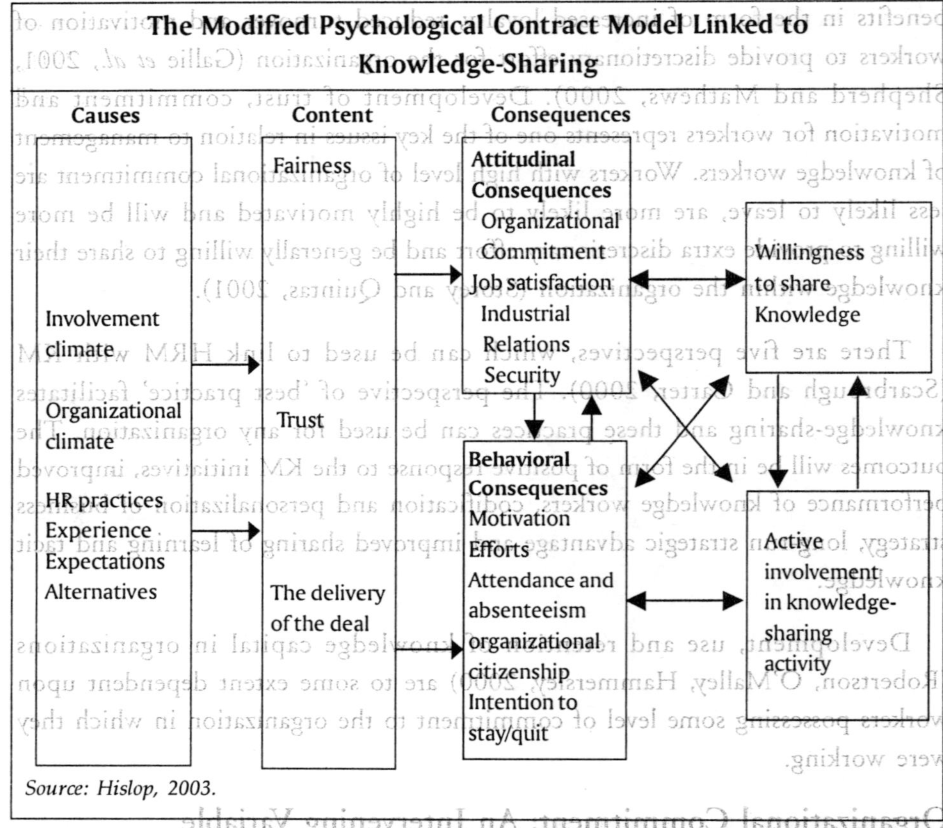

Source: Hislop, 2003.

organization and behavioral response towards KM initiatives through empirical research.

The broad objective of this paper is to take the attention of the readers from system and technology-based KM initiatives to human resource-based KM initiatives. Attitude and behavior of employees towards knowledge-sharing initiatives has its fundamental in the psychological and social-sharing initiatives in organizational context. The second idea floated in this paper is to look at a moderating variable called 'organizational commitment' that is built through best practices and HR initiatives in organizations to influence the level of knowledge sharing in organizations. A model is suggested to link HRM initiatives with organizational commitment, which influences knowledge-sharing and management in the organizations. We plan to look at the macro issues like the role of organizational climate and national/country culture as an intervening variable in our next endeavor.

(*Tapan K Panda, Professor of Marketing, Indian Institute of Management, Indore. He can be reached at tapan@iimidr.ac.in*

Tapas K Panda, Lecturer in Marketing, Institute of Management and Information Science, Bhubaneswar.

Subrat K Mishra, Chief Administrative Officer, Indian Institute of Management, Indore.)

References

1. Beaumont P and Hunter L (2002), *Managing Knowledge Workers*, CIPD London.
2. Blacker F (1995), "Knowledge, Knowledge Work and Organizations, An Overview and Interpretations", *Organization Studies*, Vol. 16, No. 6, pp.1021-64.
3. Chen Z and Francesco A (2000), "Employee Demography, Organizational Commitment, and Turnover Intentions in China: Do Cultural Differences Matter", *Human Relations*, Vol. 53, No. 6, pp. 869-87.
4. Empson L (2001), "Fear of Exploitation and Fear of Contamination: Impediments to Knowledge Transfer in Mergers between Professional Service Firms", *Human Relations*, Vol. 54, No. 7, pp. 839-62.
5. Flood P, Turner T, Ramamoorthy N and Pearson J (2001), "Causes and Consequences of Psychological Contracts among Knowledge Workers in the High Technology and Financial Services Industry", *International Journal of Human Resource Management*, Vol. 12, No. 7, pp. 1152-61.
6. Gallie D, Felstead A, Green F (2001), "Employer Policies and Organizational Commitment in Britain 1992-97", *Journal of Management Studies*, Vol. 38, No. 8, pp. 1081-97.
7. Guest D (1998), "The Role of Psychological Contract", in Perkins, S and Sandrigham, St Jr (Eds), *Trust, Motivation and Commitment: A Reader*, Strategic Remuneration Research Center, Faringdon, Oxford.
8. Guest D and Conway N (1998), *Organizational Change and Psychological Contract*, IPD, London.
9. Hislop, Donald (2003), "Linking Human Resource Management and Knowledge Management via Commitment", *Employee Relations*, Vol. 25, No. 2, pp.182-202.

10. Iversion R and Buttigeg D (1999), "Affective, Normative and Continuance Commitment: Can the Right Kind of Commitment be Managed", *Journal of Management Studies,* Vol. 36, No. 3, pp. 307-33.

11. Kim W and Mauborgne (1998), "Procedural Justice, Strategic Decision Making and the Knowledge Economy", *Strategic Management Journal,* Vol. 19, pp. 323-38.

12. Marks A (2001), "Developing a Multi-foci Conceptualization of the Psychological Contract", *Employee Relations,* Vol. 23, No. 5, pp. 454-67.

13. Robertson M and O'Malley Hammersley (1995), "Knowledge Management Practices Within a Knowledge Intensive Firm: The Significance of People Management Dimension", *Journal of European Industrial Training,* Vol. 24, No. 2-4, pp. 241-53.

14. Scarbroug H and Carter C (2000), *Investigating Knowledge Management,* CIPD, London.

15. Scarbroug, H and Swan J (1999), *Case Studies in Knowledge Management,* IPD, London.

16. Shepherd J and Mathews B (2000), "Employee Commitment: Academic Vs Practitioners Perspective", *Employee Relations,* Vol. 22, No. 6, pp. 555-75.

17. Storey J and Barnett E (2000), "Knowledge Management Initiatives: Learning From Failure", *Journal of Knowledge Management,* Vol. 4, No. 2, pp. 145-56.

18. Storey J and Quintas P (2001), "Knowledge Management and HRM", in Storey J (Eds) *Human Resource Management: A Critical Text,* Thomson Learning.

19. William P, Fenton O, Creevy M, Nicholson N and Soane E (2001), "Knowing the Risk: Theory and Practice in Financial Market Trading", *Human Relations,* Vol. 54, No. 7, pp. 11-25.

4

Emerging Global Issues in Human Resource Management

William J Rothwell and Tiffani D Payne

In the near future, HR professionals will be required to face sequential challenges in the grounds of knowledge society. These challenges may arise from their performance aspect and grow over till the employees are made true business partners. Such issues posing exciting questions to contemplate for future research and practice are discussed in this article.

Employment in a knowledge society poses unique challenges to employers, operating managers, workers, and human resource (HR) professionals around the world. While many issues may differ due to local culture, labor market conditions, and labor laws and rules—always important foundation issues for HR management—many challenges for HR practitioners remain truly global in scope. Some such challenges are: (1) launching and sustaining effective performance management systems; (2) building and maintaining effective recruitment efforts; (3) establishing and sustaining effective training and development efforts; (4) aligning reward management initiatives with individual preferences and employer strategic objectives; (5) building effective career management systems; and (6) making employees true business partners.

Launching and Sustaining Effective Performance Management Systems

Performance management deals with many organizational problems. Defining, measuring, and inciting employee performance to stimulate and maintain overall organizational performance is one of the major problems. Three key challenges have emerged in launching and sustaining effective performance management systems. The first challenge is clearly defining the term 'performance management'. The second is building and giving support for such systems. The third is keeping pace with breaking trends in performance management.

Defining the Term 'Performance Management'

An initial challenge with performance management is that the term, like so many in HR management, actually has several possible meanings. No official definition exists with which everyone agrees. That complicates discussions about it.

In one sense, performance management can mean the same thing as performance appraisal. As typically understood, a performance appraisal is an examination of a worker's performance over a fixed time span—usually one year. A performance appraisal bears a logical relationship to a job description. While a job description lists what people do in their jobs, performance appraisal assesses how well they acquitted their duties and responsibilities over a defined time (Bohlander and Snell, 2003). However, performance appraisals, in the traditional sense, have been falling out of favor (Fandray, 2001). One reason is that they are episodic and periodic rather than continuous (Weaver, 1996).

Performance management can also mean a comprehensive process that encompasses planning for future performance, tracking performance as it occurs, and rating performance at the end of a review period. In this sense, performance management covers more than mere end-of-the-cycle performance appraisal alone. Therefore, most multinational corporations use this term (Tyler, 2005). Often, performance management systems are integrated with competency models, succession plans, and work/process planning systems.

A third way to think of performance management is to regard it as synonymous with real-time performance feedback systems. Feedback gives individuals, work groups, departments, and organizations information from other people about how well the performance demonstrated matches the expected or desired performance. A real-time feedback system is thus one that gives people almost instantaneous feedback on how well their performance meets or exceeds the needs of those people who depend on it, such as the real-time customer feedback system of retailer Trader Joe's (McGregor, 2004). It is far more powerful than training as it allows real-time and continuous improvement; real-time feedback systems hold promising potential for the future ("How to Move Your Organization", 2004). Relatively little research has focused on applications of real-time feedback systems that minimize the role of third parties—such as supervisors—in the process of giving performers feedback on what they did and how well they met the expectations of those they served (Moss and Sanchez, 2004). One of the best practical examples, however, is 3M's leadership program that permits leaders to integrate many feedback systems (Jossi, 2004), but the relatively poor ability of supervisors to give workers useful feedback is leading to an epidemic in poor supervision (Tulgan, 2004). Overall, performance management can be defined as a complete work system designed to enable employees to perform to the best of their abilities.

Building and Giving Support for Performance Management Systems

Almost every HR practitioner knows that operating managers rarely regard performance management systems with enthusiasm. Indeed, introducing a new performance management system is akin to introducing a new consumer product. Few operating managers initially support any new performance management system; others regard such systems with skepticism; and many simply use it only when forced to do so.

What is needed is more research on effective approaches to building and keeping support for performance management systems. A corollary to that is to identify the key objections or problems with such systems and pinpoint the best practices in overcoming the objections and solving the problems.

Keeping Pace with Breaking Trends and Issues in Performance Management

How is worker productivity objectively measured, and how should it be measured? How much should behavior be a focus of attention in measuring performance, and how much should work outputs or outcomes be a focus of attention? How should HR systems themselves be measured, too? These key questions summarize important questions that match up to breaking trends and issues in performance management and the related topics.

Building and Sustaining Effective Recruitment Efforts

Recruitment always surges to the forefront of the attention of HR practitioners and operating managers, whenever economic conditions improve. Key challenges in recruitment are building and sustaining effective recruitment efforts both in good and bad economic times, keeping pace with e-recruitment issues, and moving beyond thinking of recruitment as an isolated effort and regarding it as an integral part of a worker socialization process that affects retention.

Building and Sustaining Effective Recruitment Efforts in Good and Bad Economic Times

It is easy to make the decision-makers to invest time, money and effort on recruitment when an organization is expanding and is facing favorable economic conditions that lead to expansion. Often, of course, good economic times mean that staffing needs are acute. More people are needed to build products, deliver services, or fill vacancies that result from the higher turnover that often goes with good economic times.

But it is not so easy to make the case for recruitment when the organization falls on hard times or when business is not so good and the organization faces cutbacks, downsizings, employee buyouts, or other efforts to cut payroll and benefit costs.

Effective recruitment efforts, however, are carried out consistently. Employers work consistently in good and bad economic times to establish and maintain an employment brand to attract the right number and type of people to meet the organization's continuous need for talent. Employers who are effective in their recruiting do not permit wild swings in recruitment investments; rather, they consistently apply them. According to the 2002 Recruiter Budge/Cost Survey, out of 278 respondent corporate recruiters, two-thirds reported a recruitment budget of up to $50,000, while one-third have more than $50,000 (Gere, Scarborough, and Collison, 2002).

They also experiment with creative approaches to recruitment because they know that, if they do only what other employers do, they will realize only the same (or worse) results than what other employers get.

Keeping Pace with E-Recruitment Issues

E-recruitment, which connotes using online and web-based approaches to recruiting people, may be one of the hottest topics in the recruiting field. Many employers are in a big rush to automate all aspects of the HR function—that includes listing openings to attract applicants faster, and often at lower cost, than through such traditional methods as newspaper advertisements, in-the-window advertisements, or other approaches. According to a study, sponsored by the Society for Human Resource Management, Gere, *et al.* (2002), utilizing the Internet to recruit employees often has no effect on the recruitment budget. In fact, according to the results of the survey (278 respondents), more than one-third say: "Their recruiting costs have decreased as a result. The most significant impact of online advertising has been broadening of the markets targeted for recruitment; a majority of respondents say use of the Internet has allowed them to recruit from a wider geographic region" (Gere *et al.*, 2002, p.2).

But e-recruitment is no panacea. Not all qualified applicants use online job searching more than they rely on any other single approach. And placing undue emphasis on one recruitment approach to the exclusion of others may not be the best way to diversify recruiting approaches to cast the broadest net to attract the best people. Additionally, even in e-recruitment, many employers have yet to determine what websites are most cost-effective for doing searches, how to set their recruitment postings apart from those of many other organizations, and how to personalize a recruitment process that can be inherently impersonal if done online.

Moving Beyond Thinking of Recruitment as Part of a Worker Socialization Process

Many managers and HR professionals regard the employment process as a series of different, and perhaps unrelated efforts. But the reality is that recruiting, selecting, orienting, and training are part of a continuing effort to socialize workers. People form impressions as they become part of an organization's corporate culture, and 'socialization' is the term we give to the gradual process of learning the culture

(Holton, 1996; Lahti *et al.*, 2002). Failures in socialization, closely related to job satisfaction (Saari and Judge, 2004), can lead to turnover statistics (Middlebrook, 1999).

Among the key questions deserving further exploration in this area are:

- How much do initial worker impressions influence subsequent socialization?
- How do people make decisions to stay or leave?
- What is the relative importance of relationships with co-workers compared to other factors?
- How can employers research the socialization process in their own organizations and mount improvement efforts to make the socialization process more successful?

Establishing and Sustaining Training and Development Efforts

Worker training has surged to the forefront of many national economic agendas for the simple reason that human capital itself can provide a nation with a comparative advantage. What can people of the nation do best? So, the question of macroeconomics is pondered by many government leaders, and the answers have important implications about what educational and workforce development investments and policy decisions may be the best to make. And what can the people of a company do best? This question of microeconomics is pondered by many business leaders, and the answers have important implications about what educational and workforce development investments of a company may be the best investments.

Three key training and development trends are worthy of consideration. First is growing attention to the role of training and development as a means of building organizational talent. Second is the movement away from training and towards an increasing focus on learning. Third is the growing attention devoted to real-time learning, and the management of it, for building competencies. Each warrants attention.

The Role of Training in Building Organizational Talent

There are only two ways to address an organization's talent needs. One is to hire from outside; the other is to train and develop people inside the organization.

For this reason, training and recruitment/selection must be integrated to meet an organization's continuing talent requirements. Gone are the days of 'manpower planning' as a way of 'planning for the headcount needed to meet production forecasts.' Today's workforce planning requires recognition that individuals differ in their abilities to be productive as well as differ qualitatively in terms of the talents they bring to their work (Dubois and Rothwell, 2004; Rothwell and Kazanas, 2003).

Training is thus important in a larger strategy to build organizational talent to meet competitive goals (Rothwell and Kazanas, 2004). Organizations like Steelcase, Inc., have made a deliberate effort to integrate talent development with other strategic goals such as using intellectual capital for innovation, identifying leadership potential, demonstrating how learning has an impact on organizational performance, and predicting the future of corporate learning (Bingham and Galagan, 2005). "According to HR professionals, the top employee development methods used by organizations encompass some form of training" (Esen and Collison, 2005, p.ix). Esen, *et al.* (2005) purport that the training methods used are: 1) generic training programs unrelated to leadership training; 2) cross-functional training; 3) leadership training; and 4) developmental planning.

Moving Away from Training and Toward Learning

Training is something that is imparted to others. But learning is something that individuals are empowered to do for themselves. Unfortunately, traditional education around the world has too often focused its most attention on the role of the teacher in guiding learning. Indeed, much attention has been devoted to the roles and competencies of trainers, but much less time and attention has been devoted to the roles and competencies of individual learners who must grapple with real-time work challenges to achieve results (Refer Rothwell, 2002). So, "while training is certainly an important component in furthering employee competencies, formal learning opportunities that provide experiential practice are also thought to be effective since such programs are directly focused on the individual" (Esen, *et al.,* 2005, p.1).

And yet the trend is to make e-learning a key to delivering training, and recent statistics reveal that about 78% of all e-learning is entirely learner-directed.

There is no teacher, trainer or facilitator. The success of the learning effort hinges entirely on the ability of the learner to make the best use of the learning resources provided to him or her. That means that, counter to the practices still demonstrated in many educational institutions, learners must become more competent in the learning process so that they can keep their knowledge, skills and abilities current as the half-life of all human knowledge dips below five years. Learning has become the focus of attention, supplanting training (Galagan, 2003). Thus, "employee development programs are of strategic importance to both organizations and employees. Organizations that offer employees opportunities to evolve and increase the likelihood of retaining their talent and, in turn, create a cadre of workers equipped to grow within the organizational structure" (Esen, *et al.*, 2005, p. 21).

Growing Attention Devoted to Real-Time Learning

While much attention has traditionally been focused on the off-the-job training, most learning actually occurs in real time and on the job. People learn as a by-product of work experience. And that is why work experience is so highly valued by employers. As many organizations move to competency-based HR systems (Dubois and Rothwell, 2004), an emerging challenge is how to link continuing work efforts with competency-building activities geared to keep an individual current, make an individual more productive, or prepare an individual for future advancement. In short, training and learning must become focused on real-time improvement (Edwards, 2005).

At the very same time, many organizations are moving toward centralizing their training functions. While years of decentralization has occurred in a bid to move training closer to operations, technology-assisted training has increasingly prompted companies like Cendant Real Estate Franchise Group, Boeing, and Schwan Foods to move their training to centralized functions (Oakes, 2005).

Aligning Reward Management Initiatives with Individual Preferences and Employer Strategic Objectives

"Employee compensation is an important component of human resource management, and reward programs and incentive compensation are an important part of an employee's compensation package" (Burke, 2005, p.vii). Because of this, employers globally are growing more sophisticated in their understanding of reward and incentive systems. Of course, a 'reward' means a positive reinforcement for performance after it is demonstrated; an 'incentive' is a promise of a reward if desired results are delivered. Employers have been experimenting with many new ways to increase productivity by the creative use of reward and incentive systems.

Two key issues about reward and incentive systems are of growing importance. One is to develop and sustain a consistent understanding of what performance means and how to measure it effectively. A second is the challenge posed in trying to achieve elegant simplicity with reward systems and yet align them with differing individual preferences and dynamically changing employer-strategic objectives.

Developing and Sustaining a Consistent Understanding of Performance and Measuring It

'Performance' in Western culture is synonymous with 'productivity'. It is what people do and the results they achieve that match up to desired results. But not all cultures in the world regard performance in exactly the same way. Indeed, in some cultures—particularly developing economies—relationships with immediate supervisors, family relationships, political affiliations, family of birth or personal friendships may outweigh objectively-measured work results in assessments of individual "performance."

What is needed is a more consistent view of worker performance and more objective ways of measuring it. In the Society for Human Resource Management study (2005 Reward Programs and Incentive Compensation), over half (52%) of the respondents surveyed indicated that measuring achievements of employees is somewhat of a challenge (Burke, 2005). Traditional check-box approaches on performance appraisal forms do not achieve the level of rigor that measuring performance deserves. Nor do they necessarily give sufficient weight in the relative importance, and relative differences, of individual performance in achieving and sustaining competitive advantage for organizations or nations (London *et al.*, 2004). Worker performance is merely a piece of the system and must be measured in conjunction with process and organization, in order to "monitor, control, and improve system performance" (Rummler and Brache, 1995, p.135).

Keeping Reward Systems Simple but Aligned with Individual Preferences and Employer-Strategic Objectives

Almost everyone likes the notion of 'pay for performance'. The devil is in the details of what that means. Obviously, notions of paying for performance will differ when notions of performance itself differ. For instance, "management is more likely than non-management to be eligible for monetary rewards based on long-term objectives such as incentive compensation, year-end bonuses and profit sharing... non-management employees are more likely... to be eligible for monetary programs such as new-hire referral bonuses and spot bonuses that recognize more short-term accomplishments" (Burke, 2005, p.viii).

Reward systems are far more complex than many people give them credit for. Ask a manager—or a worker—what is a reward, and he or she is most likely to point to an increase in wage or salary. But rewarding human performance is really much more complex than that. In other words, it is to just say how complex human behavior and perceptions can be. Not all individuals prize money in the same way or regard it in the same fashion (Arthur, 1998). For some, it is necessary for survival; for others, it may merely represent a standard for recognition.

The real challenge is to provide elegant but simple incentive systems that promise dependable rewards for specific results that matter to individuals, and that match achievement to organizational objectives. The same principle applies to reward systems. This is all the harder to do because rewards must be given for more than mere individual achievement or contributions.

They must also take into account the value of jobs in the external labor market, the value of individual contributions to group, team, division, department or organizational performance, and preserve the relationships that exist among and between jobs in an organization. Simply put, reward and incentive programs should be designed to "recognize and encourage good performance" (Burke, 2005, p.vii).

Reward systems typically fail for eight well-documented reasons (Spitzer, 1996). First, they place undue impact on monetary rewards. Second, they do not give sufficient attention to employee recognition. Third, some rewards are regarded as entitlements rather than being linked directly to productivity improvement.

Fourth, difficulties in measurement lead to rewarding the wrong things. Fifth, the lag time between performance and rewards is too long.

Sixth, rewards are generic and are not customized to what matters most to individuals. Seventh, reward systems often place undue emphasis on short-term rewards, such as money. And some reward systems make people who are not rewarded more angry than the rewards serve to stimulate productivity among those who are rewarded.

Building Effective Career Management Systems

Career management systems are now a focus of attention for several reasons. First, many organizations globally face a crisis as many experienced workers qualify for retirement with few qualified replacements in sight after years of cost-cutting efforts carried out through downsizing, contingent staffing, and outsourcing. Second, career management systems provide an important alternative to, or even a supplement for, employer succession planning and talent management programs. Third, career management systems are retention strategies, showing highly-talented workers what they must do to qualify for advancement or what they must do to develop themselves professionally to maintain employability in dynamically-changeable global labor markets.

Career Management as a Strategy to Prepare for Widespread Retirements

The world faces a crisis as a high percentage of seasoned veterans retire from business, government and non-profit firms at about the same time. Not only will that create a war for talent but may lead to a global recession as organizational leaders scramble to find replacements for people who may also possess special institutional memory that cannot easily be replaced or passed on.

Career management systems are ways to help individuals prepare for advancement. They can also show the relationships among jobs, hierarchical levels and departments in ways that can provide individuals with useful information to prepare themselves for a future that may not be like the past.

Career Management as an Alternative to Succession Planning

While many organizations are now preparing for a pending tidal wave of retirements by installing succession programs, others are struggling to sustain the long-term viability of such programs. One reason for succession planning programs to suffer is that such top-down programs do not always enjoy the long-term support and ownership of sometimes-complacent and soon-to-be-retired senior executives.

For that reason, some organizations launch career programs as a bottom-up approach to talent development. After all, career programs can prompt high potential workers to ask their immediate supervisors some tough questions about the future. Such questions may require senior leaders to make decisions, take developmental actions, and sustain attention to developing people in ways that may be nicely integrated with and supportive of succession programs (Rothwell, Jackson, Knight, and Lindholm, 2005). As one of many examples, Ernst and Young was cited for excellence in assigning a career counselor to every employee to assist in developing a learning plan and setting career goals ("Top 100", 2005). A noteworthy example is UNICEF's 'personal times professional development program', a first-rate career program (Messinger and Rothwell, 2005).

Career Management as a Retention Strategy

Career management programs can also provide a nice focal point for employer retention efforts as organizations struggle to hold down turnover. Career programs can show workers what might be in it for them to develop themselves. If properly managed, career programs can also help workers develop realistic expectations about what they must do to prepare themselves for higher-level responsibility, how to do that, and how to pursue alternatives to it such as building their competencies along a horizontal continuum of technical expertise.

Organizational leaders must recognize that individuals want different things. That means that retention strategies may need to differ by national culture, corporate culture—and generational differences (Kaplan-Leisserson, 2005). That means that effective retention strategies may need to be the result of investigation by organizational leaders to find out what people value the most—an issue that also impacts experimentation with reward systems (Babcock, 2005).

Making Employees True Business Partners

How can employers move beyond authoritarian, paternalistic or even nominally participative approaches to meet the challenges of making employees true business partners? What is meant by such terms as employee involvement and employee empowerment? What effective strategies have emerged to make employees true business partners?

What is Meant by 'Employee Involvement' and 'Employee Empowerment'

'Employee involvement' literally means to involve employees in decisions and other matters that affect them. 'Employee empowerment' goes beyond involvement to mean giving employees the power to make decisions on matters that affect them or their customers. While much has been written and spoken about both employee involvement and employee empowerment, it does not require much of a stretch of the imagination to say that actual conditions in many organizations fall far short of the potential of such efforts (Forrester, 2000; Randolph, 2000). In many places, managers still make all the key decisions and retain all the power. Little wonder that more turnover results from bad management practice than from individual employee bids to achieve higher wages (Dover, 1999).

What Strategies have Emerged as Particularly Effective in Making Employees True Business Partners?

Two major approaches have emerged as particularly effective in making employees true business partners:

One approach is a comprehensive organizational change effort designed to build a high-involvement workplace. Research has revealed much about the conditions that should exist in an organization if it is to be a High Involvement Organization (HIO) (Becker and Steele, 1995; Howard and Associates, 1994). Much of that research supports the relationship between organizations, where workers are most productive and organizations where workers are most involved and empowered (Blanger and Murray, 2002). One place to start is to measure workers' perceptions of how closely their organization matches up to the conditions associated with a high performance or high involvement workplace. Then leaders can work with Organization Development (OD) practitioners to undertake long-term change efforts that will close gaps between actual and desired conditions in the corporate culture.

Another approach is to investigate employee ownership of organizations (Rosen, Case and Staubus, 2005). In an ESOP, for instance, employees are given shares of ownership in the business. They become true shareholders and part-owners of the business. Of course, such efforts must comply with national rules of stock ownership, but at least an effort has been made to provide advice to multinational companies interested in fostering the notion of the ESOP (Equity-Based Compensation for Multinational Corporations, 1999). For more information on ESOPs, refer http://www.nceo.org.

Conclusion

Growing attention is being focused on HR. HR practitioners must become true leaders for the people side of the enterprise to help employers and workers meet these present and future challenges.

(William J Rothwell, PhD, is professor-in-charge of Workforce Education and Development in the Department of Learning and Performance Systems on the University Park Campus of The Pennsylvania State University. He is also president of his own consulting company, Rothwell and Associates, Inc. (Refer www.rothwell-associates.com) He is also the lead editor of The Encyclopedia of Human Resource Management and Workforce Policy *(Refer www.hrdictionary.com).*

Tiffani D Payne, Bunton-Waller Fellow, is PhD in Workforce Education and Development in the Department of Learning and Performance Systems on the University Park Campus of The Pennsylvania State University. She can be reached at tdp145@psu.edu).

References

1. Arthur, J (1998), "Status Cues", *Human Resource Executive,* 12(11), 80-82.
2. Babcock, P (2005), "Find What Workers Want", *HR Magazine,* 50(4), 50-56.
3. Becker, F, and Steele, F (1995), *Workplace by Design: Mapping the High-performance Workscape,* San Francisco: Jossey-Bass.
4. Bingham, T, and Galagan, P (2005), A Conversation with James P Hackett. *T + D,* 59(4), 22-26.
5. Blanger, J, and Murray, G (Eds.) (2002), *Work and Employment in the High Performance Workplace,* New York: Continuum International Publishing Group.
6. Bohlander, G, and Snell, S (2003), *Managing Human Resources,* 13th ed. Cincinnati, OH: South-Western.

7. Burke, M E (2005), 2005 *Reward Programs and Incentive Programs Survey Report,* Arlington, VA: Society for Human Resource Management.

8. Dover, K (1999), "Avoiding Empowerment Traps", *Management Review,* 88(1), 51-55.

9. Edwards, R (2005), "Knowledge Sharing for the Mobile Workforce", *Chief Learning Officer,* 4(5), 48-53.

10. *Equity Based Compensation for Multinational Corporations* (1999), 2nd ed. NCEO Oakland, CA: The National Center for Employee Owners.

11. Esen, E, and Collison, J (2005), *Employee Development Survey Report,* Arlington, VA: Society for Human Resource Management.

12. Fandray, D (2001), "The New Thinking in Performance Appraisals", *Workforce,* 80(5), 36-40.

13. Flaherty, J (2005), "Trainer as Retention Agent", *T + D,* 59(2), 61-64.

14. Forrester, R (2000), "Empowerment: Rejuvenating a Potent Idea", *Academy of Management Review,* 14(3), 67-80.

15. Galagan, P (2003), "The Future of the Profession Formerly Known as Training", *T + D,* 57(12), 26-38.

16. Gere, D, Scarborough, E K, and Collison, J (2002), 2002 *Recruiter Budget/Cost Survey,* Alexandria, VA: Society for Human Resource Management.

17. Holton, E (1996), "New Employee Development: A Review and Reconceptualization", *Human Resource Development Quarterly,* 7(3), 233-252.

18. How to Move Your Organization from Theory to Improved performance (2004, May), *IOMA's Report on Managing Training and Development,* Nos. 4-5, 6-7.

19. Howard, A and Associates (1994), *Diagnosis for Organizational Change. Methods and Models,* New York: Guilford Press.

20. Jossi, F (2004), "Stuck on Change", *Human Resource Executive,* 18(4), 16-22

21. Kaplan-Leisserson, E (2005), "The Changing Workforce", *T + D,* 59(2), 10-12.

22. Lahti, R et al. (2002), "Developing the Productivity of a Dynamic Workforce: The Impact of Informal Knowledge Transfer", *Journal of Organizational Excellence,* 21(2), 13-21.

23. London, M et al. (2004), "Performance Management and Assessment: Methods for Improved Rater Accuracy and Employee Goal Setting", *Human Resource Management,* 43(4), 319-336.

24. McGregor, J (2004, October), "2004 Fast Company Customer First Awards", *Fast Company,* 87, 79-88.

25. Messinger, R, and Rothwell, W (2005), Unicef. In L Carter, M Sobol, P Harkins, D Giber and M Tarquinio (Eds.), *Best Practices in Leading the Global Workforce: How the Best Global Companies Ensure Success throughout their Workforce* (pp. 315-330). Burlington, MA: Linkage Press.

26. Middlebrook, J (1999), "Avoiding Brain Drain: How to Lock in Talent". *HR Focus,* 76(3), 9-10.

27. Moss, S, and Sanchez, J (2004), "Are Your Employees Avoiding You? Managerial Strategies for Closing the Feedback Gap", *Academy of Management Executive,* 18(1), 32-44.

28. Oakes, K (2005), "Grand Central Training", *T + D,* 49(5), 30-32.

29. Randolph, A (2000), "Re-thinking Empowerment: Why is it So Hard to Achieve?" *Organizational Dynamics,* 29(2), 94-107.

30. Rosen, C, Case, J, and Staubus, M (2005), *Equity: Why Employee Ownership is Good for Business.* New York: Harvard Business School Press.

31. Rothwell, W (2005), *Effective Succession Planning: Ensuring Leadership Continuity and Building Talent from Within,* 3rd ed. New York: Amacom.

32. Rothwell, W (2002), *The Workplace Learner: How to Align Training Initiatives with Individual Learning Competencies,* New York: Amacom.

33. Rothwell, W, Jackson, R, Knight, S, Lindholm, J with Wang, A, and Payne, T (2005), *Career Planning and Succession Management: Developing Your Organization's Talent—For Today and Tomorrow.* Westport, CT: Greenwood Press/an imprint of Praeger.

34. Rothwell, W, and Kazanas, H (2003), *Planning and Managing Human Resources: Strategic Planning for Human Resource Management* (2nd ed.), Amherst, MA: HRD Press.

35. Saari, L, and Judge, T (2004), "Employee Attitudes and Job Satisfaction", *Human Resource Management,* 43(4), 395-407.

36. Spitzer, D (1996), "Power Rewards: Rewards that Really Motivate", *Management Review,* 85 (8), 45-50.

37. "Top 100 Best Practices" (2005), *Training,* 42(3), 68-70.

38. Tulgan, B (2004), "The Under-management Epidemic", *HR Magazine,* 49(10), 119-122.

39. Tyler, K (2005), "Performance Art", *HR Magazine,* 50(8), 58-63.

40. Weaver, W (1996), "Linking Performance Reviews to Productivity and Quality", *HR Magazine,* 41(11), 93-98.

41. Williams, R (2004), *"Tell Me How I'm Doing: A Fable About the Importance of Giving Feedback",* New York: Amacom.

5

Challenges for HR Professionals in the Knowledge-Driven Era

Rajashree Vyas

In this knowledge-driven era, change is the only constant phenomenon. This poses challenges for HRM, which could start from bringing about changes in the organization's structure, workplace, knowledge management as well as negative practices like poaching. All HRM activities need to be looked at again in order to develop an environment that fosters growth.

The affairs of the business world, today, are in a flux and evolving at a rapid pace. Rapid growth of innovations, changing legislations, growing lawsuits against firms, higher expectations, mergers and acquisitions seem to be the order of the day. To cope with this changing environment, the managers have to constantly innovate and move along at a rapid pace. Any organization not willing to adapt to these changing demands will eventually have to move out and make way for the newer and more competitive company to take its place. Darwin's theory, "survival of the fittest", holds true now.

Globalization itself has several implications, particularly in developing countries. It entails new markets, new products, new mindsets, new competencies and new ways of doing business. Hence, it is one of the main competitive challenges of human resource management (HRM). The world is becoming a small place due to globalization, with the introduction of various telecommunications, travel and information systems. The structure and operations of many industries are completely changed by globalization. Most of the enterprises have become highly transparent because of the forces like global access and information technology. The organizations have been transformed into more responsive, faster, less bureaucratic and less hierarchical firms. Sustainability of competitive advantage requires rethinking as the value-laden resources (particularly intellectual ones) have become increasingly mobile. A different type of management thinking and non-linear and innovative ways for handling human resource (HR) issues are called for. In global competition, HR functions that are patterned on an external market model begin to take shape as they operate more as "customer-centric" businesses. The stress is being put by a number of contemporary HR commentators on the need to identify and define who their customers are. Universal access to HR-related information and self-service options will be allowed by the new technology that is part of globalization process and there will be greater convenience and freedom to the customer.

The combined influence of globalization and information revolution on HRM can be explained or symbolized as a journey of transition and transformation from HR being a specialist function, practiced only by HR specialists to a function that fosters people development through knowledge management. The challenges to the HR profession in this knowledge-driven era are thus assuming new dimensions as discussed in this paper.

The Change in the Structure of Organization

The transformation from rigid hierarchical pyramids to dynamic adaptive entities is the first change in the structure of organizations. The structure shifts conceptually from inflexibility to flexibility and from fixed to fuzzy limits. As the emerging organizational structures will look quite different, the flattening of organization is only part of the journey. Knowledge, being the critical variable in these new integrated network organizations, an emerging interactive service value net is replacing the old conventional value chain giving birth to the idea of shared intellectual capital as part of the Net. As a result of this new scenario, HR shifts its focus from only-people management approach to their interaction and processes. Hence, this practice of HRM is expected to contribute to global networking.

The Change in Workplace

In many respects, nowadays, there is no requirement of definite workplace as the changing environment has moved us from linear, standardized workplace to an online network world making huge impact on management and converting it outward-looking instead of inward-looking. HR professionals are competing on sustained performance and also investments in technology and people instead of downsizing, cost-cutting and restructuring, as they used to do in the past.

Due to job insecurity, today's employees think why to commit to an employer who may shed them tomorrow? The length of service will also now actively operate against employees after performance in retention of jobs when there is a change. Hence, the employees have assumed that there is a change in contract. Due to enlightened thinking brought by HR people, all these values are evolving, but the job insecurity cannot be compensated by any amount of enlightenment.

The Change in Parameter of Evaluation

Our whole concept of value and value creation is forced to be redefined due to knowledge economy. The generation and application of knowledge is a direct input for the outcome of value creation. We are moved from finite to infinite resources with the laws of different knowledge economy. HR professionals' measurement of performance is no longer apt; this is one of the difficulties with the emerging framework.

The New Management: Knowledge Management

The new ways of managing people are proclaimed by these transformations. The intellectual capital as well as traditional stockholder capital is equally important in some organizations. As the outputs (annual reports and accounts) of the traditional accounting system are history, they do not capture intellectual capital. It's about nourishment of the future; that's what the knowledge management is about. It can be seen as the process of value creation. Human capital, structural capital and customer capital are the components of intellectual capital. The conversion of human skills into structural capital is the key challenge since human capital is the most critical.

The Future of HR

First, a different approach is required for the management of knowledge and knowledge workers. Bluntly speaking, "grabbiness" and relationship-building do not go together. Arising out of this, we come to know the importance of measurement and the use of new measures to make an assessment of intellectual capital. Some of the major areas for innovation are presented below.

Training and Development

Due to increased work pressure and stiff competition, the psychological toll on the people is at an all-time high which is affecting their relationships, culture, social contacts, alienation, withdrawal, over-dependence in a relationship, and irritability leading to a quick burnout.

Due to stiff performance criteria and constant fear of losing job, more training programs are needed to give the average performer a chance to perform and reach the desired levels of performance. Training, performance management and talent management are being seen as the next big wave.

As the organization goes global, having many offices worldwide with each country having its different languages, the training given to them is essential without getting into any language barriers, e.g., BMW plant. Each mechanic in the service centers has to be certified in servicing any new car the company brings out. If the car is serviced by any other mechanic, BMW will be liable to pay any damages arising out of it. Hence, training all the people across different countries having different languages is done by means of an e-learning package through which each employee has to log in and pass the required stage before being certified in handling the car.

Leadership Skills

These refer to the leadership skills that could manage innovation and organizational change. It can be achieved by leadership training. The success will, however, depend on inherent qualities that go into making a person a natural leader. Leadership training helps people to master the management skills.

The increasing educated workforce knows its rights and demands to know what is expected from it. Due to this kind of awareness, exploitation of employees by the management has been reduced to a great extent.

Poaching

Poaching is the main concern as the demand for skilled manpower goes up, especially at the top spots. Rival companies are offering pay packages @ 50% – 100% more than the existing ones. This is especially true in case of sunrise sector like aviation. In this information era, getting talented people and managing them is the need of the hour.

Pay–Performance Relation

It refers to matching the pay with performance and bringing about a performance-oriented reward system, like the one being used by TCS by means of Economic Value Add (EVA).

It aims at creating a perfect work-life balance so that employees do not think they are being burdened with more work.

Golden handcuffs, wherein companies tend to create deferred compensation to retain hotshots, cool-off period for joining direct competition, formal and informal non-poaching agreements as well as relieving letter or no-objection letter, are being worked out. The main problem here is that a violation of non-poaching agreement doesn't carry much legal weight. It facilitates further education of employees and develops a talent pool of internal employees to source from, whenever there is a requirement of internal vacancies. This will act as a good motivator for people working with the organization. To develop this, many organizations have tied up with leading educational institutions across the country and offer an MBA degree to their employees.

E Motivation

Measuring the various HR initiatives will be very necessary to see the effectiveness in the company. Motivation is no longer by means of a fat pay cheque, hence newer methods of motivation have to be thought about. Giving people meaningful work and making them feel that what they do really make a difference.

Organizations are coming up with alternate work schedule instead of the regular 9 – 5 job timings. Creating a culture in the organization wherein each employee feels a part of it will be of utmost importance, since they would require more than money to stay put at that place and stop employee migration from one place to another.

Conclusion

HR professionals' role is no longer restricted to just administration and recruitment. The future of HR is slowly shifting from support function to more of a strategic partner which helps the organization to achieve its objectives.

The delivery of education for HR subjects should change from the traditional approach through books to a more direct exposure from industry interface by means of a professional from industry delivering the inputs. Also, detailed and innovative methods in various areas should be included in the syllabus to make it more and more meaningful. Measuring HR activities should also be given higher priority.

The professional organizations/bodies through their latest and updated research can help the academia get a talented pool of people who could start contributing to the organization immediately.

(Dr. Rajashree Vyas is a faculty member, the ICFAI Business School, Mumbai.)

Section II

KM Issues

6

Harnessing Tacit Knowledge in Organizations

Daniel Ashish and S Senthil Kumar

The success of any organization greatly depends on management of knowledge. Such knowledge should be shared among the members of the organization. In this perspective, explicit knowledge is easy to transmit than tacit knowledge. Harnessing tacit knowledge calls for suitable HR interventions in organizations.

The eminent management thinker Peter F Drucker predicted that in the 21st century, companies would compete with one another by using their knowledge and the major challenge before the managers would be in managing the collective knowledge of the organization effectively. The knowledge base should be managed in such a way that it develops at a pace to match the current challenges of business environment, encourages all the members to contribute to it as well as benefit from it. Above all, it cannot be easily utilized by the competitors. Each person should make use of the best and most current knowledge. In order to support such knowledge-sharing systematically, many companies have adopted knowledge management practices and implemented worldwide knowledge management systems by utilizing global communication networks and groupware technology. This article first discusses knowledge base as a source of competitive advantage followed by the issues of harnessing tacit knowledge in organizations.

Source: HRM Review, November, 2004.

Knowledge Base: Source of Competitive Advantage

Knowledge-based business organizations sell their knowledge on the selected line of business in the market for a price. For example, a mutual fund company sells its knowledge (expertise) on financial management and a pharmaceutical company sells its drug formula. The knowledge manifests itself in an innovative product, efficient production process, and better utilization of human resource or market intelligence in manufacturing organizations.

The vast size of modern global enterprises, the speed with which the markets move, the increased knowledge of clients, customers, and competitors, and increased demands for personalization and specialization in products and services all demand that organizations be smarter than ever before. Moreover, organizations today operate in an increasingly complex world that requires them to apply large amounts of knowledge to their activities. Managing knowledge is crucial to organizational success. Earlier, knowledge management itself was not very important in an organization. In the information era, knowledge needs to be managed overtly. In the global economy, knowledge is a company's greatest advantage.

In the prevailing competitive landscape, traditional sources of advantage have become less relevant. Organizational advantages are rarely derived from superior technologies, distribution efficiencies, or from other value-chain activities. Rather, competitive advantages are more likely to stem from the knowledge that the organization can bring to bear on its critical activities. In order to achieve sustainable competitive advantage, the strategy should be based on the organization's knowledge base.

The organization's ability to acquire, integrate, maintain, develop and use the knowledge base is important to build sustainable competitive advantage. Effective management of knowledge base is possible only when members of the organization create new knowledge and share it with other members rapidly and widely within the organization.

Two Dimensions of Organizational Knowledge

Tacit Knowledge vs. Explicit Knowledge

Organizational knowledge—the ability to accomplish tasks that will create value to the stakeholders of the organization—has two dimensions.

"Explicit" or codified knowledge refers to knowledge that is recordable, articulable and transmittable by using systematic means. Explicit knowledge is the structured one. It is much easier to comprehend and be aware of. Organization's explicit knowledge is found in engineering drawing, procedure manuals, patents, and computer databases. Modern advancements in information and communication technology are capitalized in capturing and sharing explicit knowledge in organizations. For instance, information about market size and regulations in an overseas market can be concretely transferred to a report that can be shared within the organization. By drawing analogy between knowledge base of an organization and an iceberg, we can say that the explicit form of knowledge is only the tip of the iceberg but tacit knowledge is largely hidden and huge in size and potential.

"Tacit" or implicit knowledge, is individual-oriented and difficult to share. Tacit knowledge includes judgment, intuition, deep understanding and feelings of the members of the organization. Tacit knowledge is an essential part of "knowing how" and "knowing why" and is essential in making knowledge useful to the organization. Tacit knowledge is highly personalized and accumulated through personal experiences. Moreover, it is inside-locked and inimitable until the people reveal to others. Tacit knowledge is generally not easy to structure and explain. Consider, for instance, a quality control engineer, through years of experience, can identify the quality of a newly manufactured engine by its very sound and vibrations. Such knowledge cannot be transferred through a written document but is of great importance to the organization.

Figure 1: Explicit Knowledge Represents Only the Tip of the Iceberg (Knowledge Base) *vis-à-vis* Tacit Knowledge, Which is Largely Hidden

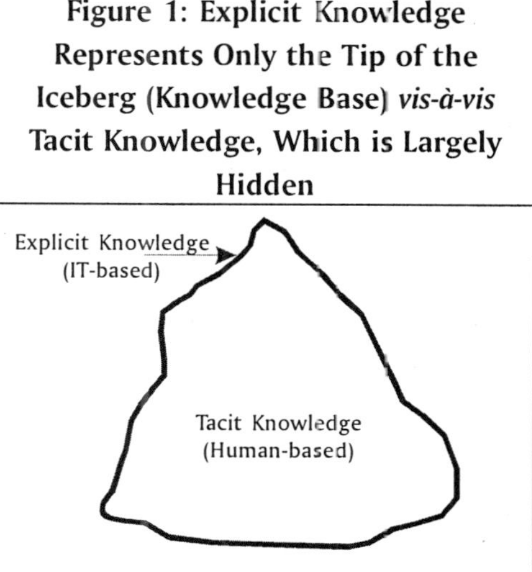

Issues in Sharing Tacit Knowledge

Knowledge is of no use to anyone unless it is shared. As mentioned above, explicit knowledge is easier to transfer and share than tacit knowledge. This makes tacit knowledge more valuable and the issue of "how to harness tacit knowledge in an organization" becomes an important one.

Two pertinent questions come to one's mind when the issue of sharing tacit knowledge crops up. First, how employees can be induced to share inherent knowledge and the second, how a knowledge-sharing culture can be built in the organizations. Both the issues have to be seen in the light of the inherent human tendency to hoard rather than share knowledge. Knowledge is mostly used as a base of power in organizations.

Encouraging Employees to Share Knowledge

Many thoughts come to our mind as we think of the process of knowledge-sharing. How many of us would want to do something for somebody for no consideration? We are sure many of us would! Now, how many of us would want to keep doing things for somebody for no consideration?

I am sure not many of us would want to. Many of our transactions, whether financial or relational or professional in nature, are based on cost-benefit analysis. As long as equilibrium is maintained between cost and benefit, we continue to engage in those transactions. Since, one of the sources of power for an individual is expertise that he/she possess, sharing the source (knowledge) may be perceived as losing some amount of power. As a result, the very idea of knowledge-sharing may be frowned upon. It is, therefore, important to back knowledge transfer activities with appropriate incentives, rewards and above all an organization culture that encourages such sharing behavior.

Incentives

Incentives that can be used by organizations to encourage knowledge-sharing must include rewards, creating appropriate conditions and infrastructure. Rewards can be of the hard and soft types. The hard type may include financial rewards, career advancement and security, access to more information and knowledge. The soft or intangible rewards can in the form of enhanced reputation and personal satisfaction. The choice between hard and soft type of incentives depends on the organizational factors.

Building Knowledge-Sharing Culture

Having the right tools and systems in place will not be of much help in an organization if such efforts are not backed by the culture that encourages knowledge transfer. We will look at how one can build and maintain a culture of knowledge sharing in the organization. Tacit knowledge, by its very nature, is complex, subtle, internalized and very difficult to externalize. An individual who possesses tacit knowledge will often find it difficult, if not impossible, to articulate such knowledge. Tacit knowledge transfers generally require extensive personal contacts. Therefore, the kind of culture that will encourage knowledge transfer can be built by adopting the following strategies.

Building Knowledge Map

The greater the size of an organization, the more the probability that the knowledge we need exists within the company. However, it simultaneously decreases the chances of our knowing who possess it, and how and where to find it. One way to overcome the difficulty in locating knowledge source is to build knowledge maps. Knowledge maps, the "Yellow Pages" of knowledge directory, point to sources where knowledge is available in the organization. Knowledge seekers can refer to knowledge maps to locate the knowledge sellers who know best about the issue concerned. This avoids "satisficing", where employees settle for "good enough" knowledge from someone in the next cubicle, than reaching the right person in another country.

Knowledge map plays an important role in facilitating the right knowledge being transferred to the right person. But building such maps requires an organized effort throughout the organization.

Capturing Tacit Knowledge

Let's envision a situation where an organization has an immaculate knowledge map in place and people know whom to go for which information. But when the knowledge buyer goes to the knowledge seller, he finds the seller is busy and cannot help him out at that time, or let's say he is on leave or even worse he has left the organization. There is no one else who has the knowledge that the knowledge buyer is seeking; what then? To avoid getting into such a tight spot organizations should try to capture, codify and document tacit knowledge so that it will be available to the organization for ever. Another way is to transfer as much knowledge as possible to other people through mentoring or apprenticeship. Multimedia computing can also be used to this purpose.

Just Talk

It is said that common sense is not very common in these days. One of the simplest ways in which tacit knowledge can be harnessed in organizations is to let their employees interact freely in an informal atmosphere. Social interactions are the most effective way of harnessing tacit knowledge. Casual atmosphere created during social interactions put people at ease, effective articulation and listening result in the process of tacit knowledge-sharing. Organizations can find innovative ways to create such occasions and encourage employees to interact with one another. From formal meetings to casual talks in the cafeteria, from knowledge fairs to open forums, each of these methods is a sure way to transfer knowledge in organizations. This apart, appropriate infrastructure should be created with adequate techno-support in the form of intranets and hobby groups.

Managing Inhibitors

A number of cultural factors inhibit knowledge transfer. These inhibitors delay or prevent the transfer of knowledge. The following are some of the common inhibitors that a company needs to overcome in order to nurture a culture of knowledge transfer.

1. Lack of trust
2. Different cultures, vocabularies and frames of references
3. Lack of time and meeting places
4. Status and rewards go to knowledge owners
5. Lack of absorptive capacity among recipients
6. "Not-invented here" syndrome
7. Intolerance for mistakes.

Thus by building the right organization culture and encouraging employees to share their knowledge, a company can transform itself into an organization that generates and uses knowledge, one that interacts with the environment, absorbs information, turns it into knowledge and takes action based on it, in combination with their experience, values and internal rules—a knowledge organization.

Conclusion

Today, on an average, about 75% of companies' market value stems from their knowledge assets in the form of intellectual capital—patents, copyrights, trade secrets, financial records, business strategies and the overall know-how. Thus, the companies need to manage their knowledge base effectively in order to achieve sustainable competitive advantage in the market.

Companies which are agile in continuously creating, disseminating new knowledge and transforming the knowledge into improved products, processes, strategies will definitely have a cutting-edge over others in competitive scenario.

Harnessing tacit knowledge in organizations calls for suitable HR interventions. HR programs and policies can be strategically aligned to the goal of harnessing tacit knowledge of the employees. One such powerful HRM tool is compensation system and it should be designed in a way that motivate employees to share their knowledge freely with others. HR interventions should be aimed at creating a learning organization where people should feel no hesitation in sharing their knowledge with others as well as seeking knowledge from others. Any successful initiative to harness tacit knowledge needs to break psychological barriers rather than organizational ones.

(Daniel Ashish is faculty member, the ICFAI Business School, Hyderabad.

S Senthil Kumar is doctoral research fellow, the ICFAI Institute for Management Teachers, Hyderabad.)

References

1. Manish Pharasi, Nihar Pradhan, *Knowledge Management,* Quality circle forum of India, May, 2000.
2. Chun Wei Choo, Nick Bontis, *The Strategic Management of Intellectual Capital and Organizational Knowledge*, Oxford University Press, 2002.

7

Recruiting Knowledge Workers

Karen Unwin

Recruitment is a key component of an organizational development (OD) strategy, but is it being treated as such? In most organizations the answer is 'no'. Recruitment is often handled by line managers who are far removed from the OD strategy. They may get expert assistance to define competency models or design assessment centers, but especially in case of knowledge workers, the relationship among recruitment, the business strategy and organizational culture is so intertwined that it must not be treated as a 'stand-alone' activity. We must also ask ourselves what skills we are recruiting for. High performance from individuals and groups is not solely dependent on professional or technical capabilities, but rather the degree of commitment to the task on hand. What, on the surface, seems like a simple subject is, in fact, multi-layered and complex.

What Kind of an Organization are We?

There is no 'one-size-fits-all' strategy to recruit, retain and incentivize high-quality knowledge workers. As ever, the first part of call must be the objectives of the organization and the culture that are to be achieved within.

Source: HRM Review, October, 2005.

Do your business objectives rely on building a workforce of high caliber, committed employees and retaining their knowledge within the company, or do you need access to a pool of high caliber contract staff for short-term projects? Yes, in both cases you will want 'high caliber' workers; your aim is always going to be to recruit productive workers who will strive to achieve the business goals; and your strategy, however, will differ greatly.

In the latter case, employing experts on short-term projects, reputation comes to the fore. By knowledge workers, we mean workers with specialized knowledge who are often part of one or more networks connected to their particular field. If you are a frequent employer you will have a reputation, good, bad or indifferent, and the best specialists want to work with employers with the best reputation. Do you know what reputation your company has among your pool of potential contractors? Is it one which will attract specialists who want to sustain their own name for professionalism and excellence? If you want to attract the best contractors then you need to offer them more than money—you need to, at least, satisfy their need to maintain their own reputation. Make no mistake, the best contractors pick and choose where they want to work, and adding another value-creating section to their résumé is only one of their needs that they will want to satisfy.

Perhaps, your business success depends on attracting and retaining talented specialists and that success will be jeopardized by frequent staff changes as knowledge leaves the company. If you are not able to retain the expertise on which you have spent so much effort on recruiting, then you must recognize that the company culture and reward structures may not support top knowledge workers' needs. Or do you need to challenge business myths regarding retention and commitment? Does commitment really take a long time to generate? According to Todd L Pittinsky and Margaret J Shih, "knowledge nomads" frequently form attachments and commit to employers when they stop.[1] Knowledge workers commit to their employers, and produce high-quality work, when their personal needs are met by working with a particular project or organization. An analysis of 49 studies on group performance, dating between 1952 and 1991,[2] concluded that commitment to the group task was the key driver of group performance, and commitment occurs when the individual's objectives are aligned to those of the group. So we must ask ourselves:

"What do Knowledge Workers Want?"

We have already touched on the subject of 'employability'; it is a primary concern of knowledge workers that they are learning and developing with every role they take. This need to be employable touches the fundamental levels of Maslow's Hierarchy of Needs; without employability, the knowledge workers cannot pay their mortgage and, even in most Western societies this does not mean homelessness; it nevertheless touches a deeply held need for security of dwelling. With such a need, high salaries alone will not keep somebody at a workplace long if they connect the job to possible homelessness!

Another factor at work is the 'Generation X' effect; more and more people are recognizing the need for a fulfilling life. Personal fulfillment takes many forms; for some, it is spending time with family, for others it is seeing the world or engaging in a sport or hobby. What each of these have in common is the need for 'time ownership'; people need to manage their own time and not be bound by models of work which originated for the efficient organization of manual labor.

People are also searching for fulfillment through the work that they do. Peter Drucker, who first coined the term 'knowledge worker' as far back as 1969,[3] says:

> What motivates workers—especially knowledge workers—is what motivates volunteers. Volunteers, we know, have to get more satisfaction from their work than paid employees precisely because they do not get a pay check. They need, above all, challenge. They need to know the organization's mission and to believe in it. They need continuous training. They need to see results. Implicit in this is that employees have to be managed as associates, partners—and not in name only.

Another observation from Peter Drucker illustrates the need for fulfillment through the workplace; "Knowledge workers don't believe they are paid to work 9 to 5; they believe they are paid to be effective."[4] A model of organization that tries to fit people, in all their wonderful diversity of skills and motivations, into tightly defined roles, will not allow them to be fully effective. However, a model that recognizes people's strengths and creates roles where they can employ those strengths, will allow them to be as effective as they can, and want to be.

It seems to me that the success or failure of creating the environment that engages employees, offers challenge and opportunity for development, allows workers to employ their strengths where they can be most effective, and has reward systems that are meaningful, depends on the leadership and management skills of the organization. Here is another part of the jigsaw—the OD strategy must include developing managers to manage knowledge workers. In addition, the processes and reward systems must be appropriate to the needs of today's workers, not yesterday's.

What Competencies are We Looking for?

Having discussed the needs of knowledge workers and the organizational models that will attract the best and generate their commitment, we now need to ask the question 'who are the best?'

One of the most well-known models of the competencies needed within a successful learning organization (and any organization employing knowledge workers must surely be a learning organization) was made popular by Senge through his influential book *The Fifth Discipline.*

Senge's five 'disciplines'[5] are:

1. Personal mastery—the ability to continually clarify and deepen a personal vision.
2. Mental models—the ability to understand one's internal maps and hold them to scrutiny.
3. Building a shared vision—the ability to develop a focus on mutual purpose.
4. Team learning—this discipline encompasses many capabilities, e.g., conflict management, facilitation, respect for other's point of view, all needed to create common learning.
5. Systems thinking (the fifth discipline)—the ability to recognize the systemic processes at work, the interdependency and complex relationships.

One of the things that the first and the second disciplines are asking of individuals within a 'learning organization' is a high level of emotional intelligence.

Daniel Goleman, who coined the term, said, "It is emotional intelligence that creates successful businesses."[6] Goleman identified five emotional and social competencies,[6] which would be needed, to some degree by all, to achieve the capabilities described by Senge.

- Self-awareness: Knowing what we are feeling at the moment and using that knowledge to guide our decision-making. Having a realistic assessment of our own abilities.
- Self-regulation: Handling our emotions so that they help us achieve our goals rather than derail us from them.
- Motivation: Use our deepest values and beliefs (our sense of identity) to help us set and achieve our goals.
- Empathy: Understanding the emotions of others and being able to take their perspective.
- Social skills: Cultivating rapport with others, reading social situations and interacting smoothly.

In effect, what is being asked of individuals is a higher order of consciousness which enables us not just to understand and obey a value system, but to create and manage our own. Kegan[7] identified six competencies being demanded of us that all require the ability to recognize, create and manage boundaries and value systems:

- Invent and own our own work (rather than see it as owned and created by the employer).
- To be self-initiating, self-correcting and self-evaluating (rather than dependent on others to frame the problems, initiate adjustments, or determine whether things are going acceptably well).
- To be guided by our own visions at work (rather than be without a vision or captive of the authority's vision).
- To take responsibility for what happens to us at work externally and internally (rather than see our present internal circumstances and future external possibilities as caused by somebody else).

- To be accomplished masters of our own particular work roles, jobs or careers (rather than having an apprenticing or imitating relationship to what we do).
- To conceive of the organization from the 'outside in' as a whole; to see our relation to the whole; to see the relation of the parts to the whole (rather than see the rest of the organization and its parts only from the perspective of our own part, from the 'inside out').

Whichever model we prefer, it seems clear that recruiting for specific technical or professional skills is not enough. Individuals with the capabilities described by Senge, Goleman and Kegan will be able to quickly align their individual goals with those of the organization, motivate themselves to achieve high levels of productivity and manage any conflicting needs from outside of the workplace.

Competency Testing

The area of competency definition and testing is one where HR practitioners can add enormous value to an organization. A properly constructed recruitment process can significantly increase the probability of a successful fit between candidate and employer. The first step in the process is to define a competency model or role for the individual. As we have discovered, we need certain personal qualities, 'emotional intelligence', to achieve high levels of performance from individuals, in addition to their professional skills. A complete model will define both sets of abilities, and the recruitment process must be designed to test them all.

The job advertisement is an opportunity to both publicize the desirable working practices of your organization, and allow candidates to self-select in or out. The latter point is especially important if you have many applicants for a single position; the more unsuitable candidates you can help to self-select out of the process, the more easily you will be able to identify really good candidates.

The first stage in the process, where it is possible to test for competencies, is the application form and/or curriculum vitae, or résumé. This is the place where professional qualifications can provide evidence of skills, and job history and personal activities can provide evidence of self-motivation.

It may be desirable, if the cost can be justified, to introduce psychometric testing to the recruitment process. This should never be used as a pass/fail test but instead as a way of gathering information which can be considered against other information gathered.

The most important competency testing technique, and the one which will be the most cost-effective, is the structured interview. Time spent creating questions which test all the identified competencies, and training interviewers to use them will provide a high return on investment.

Knowledge workers are expensive, especially those of high caliber, and creating an environment to support high productivity will take considerable time and effort. The value that can be added by a competency-based recruitment process is high... and the cost of not doing so is equally high.

The Field of Dreams: If You Build It, They Will Come

I started this article by stating that recruitment is a key component of organizational strategy. Your recruitment strategy is inextricably entwined with other parts of your OD strategy; reward systems, management skills and working practices being just a few of the dependencies. The culture of your organization may support the retention of knowledge workers by treating them as associates and partners, or you may have the difficult task of culture change to add to the OD mix. Above all, I am suggesting that organizations must focus on commitment, not retention, to ensure that the knowledge workers they recruit, whether for short-term projects or as long-term partners, are highly productive. Commitment does not necessarily take a long time to create; the more needs that can be met, the greater the commitment and the quicker it is generated.

However, you must recruit people who have the emotional skills to become committed in the first place. If you are able to achieve all of the necessary steps, you will have created an environment where the best knowledge workers want to work, and to stay. Your reputation will be high and so will the quality of your applicants.

Endnotes

1 Pittinsky T and Shih M, "Knowledge Nomads: Organizational Commitment and Worker Mobility in Positive Perspective," *American Behavioral Scientist,* February 2004.

2 Mullen B & Copper C, The Relation Between Group Cohesiveness and Performance: An Integration, *Psychological Bulletin* Vol 115, No 2., American Psychological Association, 1994.

3 Drucker P, *The Age of Discontinuity,* Harper and Row, 1969.

4 Drucker P, *Managing Knowledge Means Managing Oneself,* Leader to Leader, No. 16, Spring 2000.

5 Senge P, *The Fifth Discipline,* Doubleday, 1990.

6 Goleman D, *Working With Emotional Intelligence,* Bloomsbury Publishing, 1998.

7 Kegan R, In *Over Our Heads. The Mental Demands of Modern Life,* Harvard University Press, 1994.

(Karen Unwin has over twenty years of experience as a knowledge worker, and manager of knowledge workers, having developed her career from computer programmer to product development manager at a broadband Internet provider. After completing her MBA, Karen made a career change, retrained in neuro linguistic programming and now has a 'portfolio career'; and lecturing, coaching and training in a variety of subjects from leadership and performance skills to marketing. Karen is currently involved in recruiting, training and coaching future traders for a global trading company, Brighteye Performance Limited, UK, and has designed and implemented a recruitment process, assessment center and training program for graduates new to trading. She can be reached at karen@brighteye.co.uk).

8

Retaining Talent in Knowledge Economy

Gurdeep S Hora

Talented professionals are rewarded more in the era of knowledge economy. HR Heads are also responding through conscious and specific people-management strategies to improve the overall organizational performance. These days, job rotation and multitasking have become introductory elements of excitement and challenges in the jobs at the organizations. In such a scenario, acquisition of talent and retention would emerge as the key driver of all HR initiatives in the knowledge economy.

Today, India is at the threshold ... the threshold of an irreversible change. What we see is no more a hesitant India. A paradigm shift is taking place in the mindsets of intellectuals and intelligentia as the canvas of ideas is expanding across boundaries and we are able to view scenarios and opportunities on a global scale.

While multinational organizations, with well-defined processes and practices, are trying to expand their foothold in the country, the Indian industry has woken up to the need for benchmarking its practices and standards of performance and efficiency in line with the global competition.

Source: HRM Review, October, 2005.

It's no longer a one-time exercise. The companies have to constantly monitor performance and environment on a proactive basis and respond promptly. The emerging imperatives are for greater deliberation, analysis and evolving of systems in all areas of operations including strategic human resource management. As the knowledge and its application takes the center-stage of all economic activity and resource planning, the evolution, longevity and retention of knowledge is the key to success. Therefore, today, more than ever before, the top managements have to realize the fragility of human capital and make thorough strategic plans for retention of knowledge workers.

And it's not only an Indian phenomenon; organizations the worldover are striving to develop their people and evolve systems to constantly deliver improved performance in all areas of their operations. Today, they are not only wanting to learn from history but also proactively seeking an objective knowledge of current industry standards, trends and best practices to develop a comprehensive understanding of how competitors are addressing the key issues governing the operational performance, effectiveness and results.

The recent history of a large number of traditional Indian companies that have failed to realize this grim reality is obvious to all. The number of once-leading-companies that are now dead or dying is increasing rapidly. There is little doubt today that performance of organizations is critically linked to the quality and performance of its human resources. No organization can afford the depletion of its assets of talented performers. While machinery and other resources can be refurbished and augmented comparatively easily, knowledge workers are much more difficult to replace.

The Opportunities are Multiplying

Since the beginning of the new millennium, almost every CEO and director that we met had lamented the dearth of talented and committed professionals and their short lifespans in organizations.

Talent is fragile and needs to be handled with care. We are going through a period where exceptional talent and success get exceptional adulation. The heroes are headhunted and sought after with vengeance. While earlier

Executive Search Consultants (ESCs) were engaged for top level positions only, the trend is slowly emerging to seek specialists and niche-area professionals also through this route.

It is not a paradox that even in a confident economy where companies are giving liberal increments and there is an increasing emphasis on issues of retention. The reality of a growing economy coupled with the all-pervading sentiment of optimism about the near future has made it mandatory for the organizations to hold on to their top performers at any cost. Similarly, the availability of software and other professionals may look adequate on the surface, but due to the shift towards greater experience in niche skills, organizations are still not able to hire the right professionals.

The dearth of 'talent' persists. Thus, the focus has slowly shifted from 'numbers' to 'quality' and from 'recruitment' to 'retention', from 'training' to 'developing', and from 'guiding' to 'challenging'.

The Shifting Fulcrum

In the knowledge economy, the fulcrum has shifted towards talented professionals. Today, they feel the need to continually recharge their executives who can proactively respond to the changing market dynamics. This has suddenly brought into focus the growing importance of HR as a direct business management resource instead of merely being a people management Tool. The HR heads are responding through conscious and specific people-management strategies to improve the organizational performance. Our recent interaction with the top echelons of human resource management function in India and abroad has revealed a greater interest in knowing the best practices and strategies of successful organizations as the traditional employee satisfaction surveys are no longer able to predict retention of high-performing professionals. 'Satisfaction' is not the keyword anymore, but 'challenge' is. Without exception, the HR heads exhibited a marked anxiety to understand and implement best practices for retaining talented professionals, assessing and rewarding for exceptional performance and in developing focused compensation and benefits strategies to contribute their mite in this uncertain business environment.

There was clearly a need to further track the strategic aspects of these key business and human resource initiatives in the Indian context. So, we revisited a large number of senior HR professionals during the past few months to understand their perspectives, strategies and practices. We spent time with them in not only getting their answers to the host of questions and factors that coalesce to form the retention jigsaw puzzle but also probed and analyzed their responses with them.

The Top Five

As per our study, the top five strategies being employed by a successful company to retain its employees are as follows:

1. Provide job challenges.
2. Provide an open environment and culture.
3. Give a 'competitive' compensation.
4. Clarity of job responsibilities and career paths.
5. Continuous training and skill upgradation.

Job Challenges

The focus is back on the job and almost 65% of the CEOs and heads of HR function surveyed have ranked "providing job challenges" as one of their top two strategies for retention of employees as well as for creating a high-performance, result-oriented organization.

Some of the key elements of creating job challenges include a conscious focus on job enrichment, clarity of expectations of results, proactively encouraging innovation and creativity and empowering professionals to take decisions and risks.

The industry-wise figures indicate that this is the most crucial strategy being employed to retain top performers. The software and telecom industries swear by their jobs! However, service industries like hotels and call centers, and some of the sales-driven FMCG companies, did not give it the top rank as they felt that the highly repetitive functions of some of their employees limited the scope for providing real-job challenges. Therefore, they have to concentrate on other parameters.

Many organizations are thinking of regular job rotation and multitasking to introduce elements of excitement and challenges in the jobs. Another methodology being favored by companies in the software and telecom sector is to provide higher responsibilities early in the career to create challenging situations. However, the feeling in the consumer, engineering and chemical industries is that early promotions to positions of high responsibilities can create problems of balance in their highly structured organizations.

Organization Culture

Smart companies build an open and free organizational environment and culture that people just can't think of leaving! How they are able to accomplish this is based upon a genuine effort to understand the key needs of their employees, and not through fancy benefits and perquisites schemes.

An open culture is characterized by free channels of two-way communication. While the organization communicates its business objectives and approach to employees, they have ample opportunities to raise and discuss with superiors the issues of concern to them. The company openly shares its achievements, as well as its failures, with employees to build a relationship of trust and confidence. A display of strong business ethics by the organizations and complete transparency and honesty in human resource policies is a major contributor towards retention of high-performance employees. A strong brand image helps.

Over 52% of the companies surveyed ranked this as one of their two top business strategies to satisfy, motivate and retain their employees. Software, telecom, consumer industries, particularly MNCs, emphasized greater empowerment, delegation and risk-taking as a policy.

Good Compensation

Money matters. It still does. A good competitive compensation was ranked third in importance as a retention strategy. However, only 29% respondents treated good compensation as one of their top two strategies for retention.

Almost 45% of the organizations didn't feel that an "excellent compensation" is a prerequisite for employee retention. While half the organizations felt that salary should be according to the market value of the people, the other half were non-committal. Nobody felt that you could retain employees for long by paying them lower than their market value. 80% of the organizations felt that employees should be additionally given monetary reward by linking it to their performance on the job, while 60% felt that we must focus on giving social respect and recognition independent of the compensation or monetary rewards.

Clarity of Role and Expectations

Today, a professional expects complete clarity and understanding of the job responsibilities and management expectations of performance and results. The organizations are focusing on clearly spelling out the jobs and career paths for all. They are also redefining the Key Result Areas periodically and continually counsel and guide employees to take their feedback. The best benchmarking organizations communicate their business goals and targets in depth to the employees so that they can align their objectives and jobs in line with the organizational goals.

Overall, about 24% of the respondents treated it as one of their top two retention strategies. The focus on clarity of job responsibilities, key resulting area and career paths was maximum in FMCG (41%) followed by the manufacturing sector (15%).

Training and Development

While 100% of the respondents felt continuous training and skills development is one of the top strategies for retaining employees, only one company called it as their No.1 strategy. The focus in the software industry is naturally on technical skills training with limited stress on behavioral aspects. The consumer industry is primarily focusing at sales or marketing skills development. The HR heads were not sure if training alone can make employees stay longer and almost 50% felt that employees will leave, when they have to, irrespective of the extent or nature of training provided by the company.

The Cultural Divide

A study of responses by the companies, grouped together on the basis of their country of origin, doesn't show any drastic variations; however, some elements of differences in perception stand out.

The focus in Japanese companies is more on processes and training of employees and there is a greater commitment to retention of employees. The Japanese companies aren't sure about the role of the families in the retention of employees, while the European and Indian companies have shown a strong inclination towards involvement of families in their retention strategies. Similarly, only 50% of the Japanese companies say that they give rewards directly linked with the performance, and almost half the companies do not any longer consider job security or life-time employment as a critical policy. Compensation is an almost equally important aspect for all, but, most of the Japanese companies do not feel that monetary rewards should be given frequently. Their greater focus for motivation is on building an enabling organization culture, communication and social respect and recognition.

Unlike others, a large number of European companies do not feel that building the brand image of the company goes a long way in retaining people. However, almost all the companies felt that display of strong business ethics is very important.

The Retention Process

While many organizations use robust, structured and systematic techniques to attract and retain their customers, it is only now that many of them are applying similar methodology to retain their employees.

The process begins from the recruitment stage and continues thereafter. They need to communicate to the candidates not only the role and expectations of the management but also the cultural values of the organization to convey their emphasis on participation, motivation and involvement in decision-making. They look for employees who can shoulder responsibilities and then provide them with tools and authority to serve their internal/external customers. The focus is on systematically communicating and keeping in touch with employees and encouraging innovation and ingenuity, while providing opportunities to upgrade their skills.

It is a reality that most effective employee-retention strategies are almost cost free. Then, why the majority of Indian organizations are still not focusing on employee satisfaction and performance with the same aggressive emphasis as some of the successful multinational organizations.

The Career and Performance Enhancement Continuum

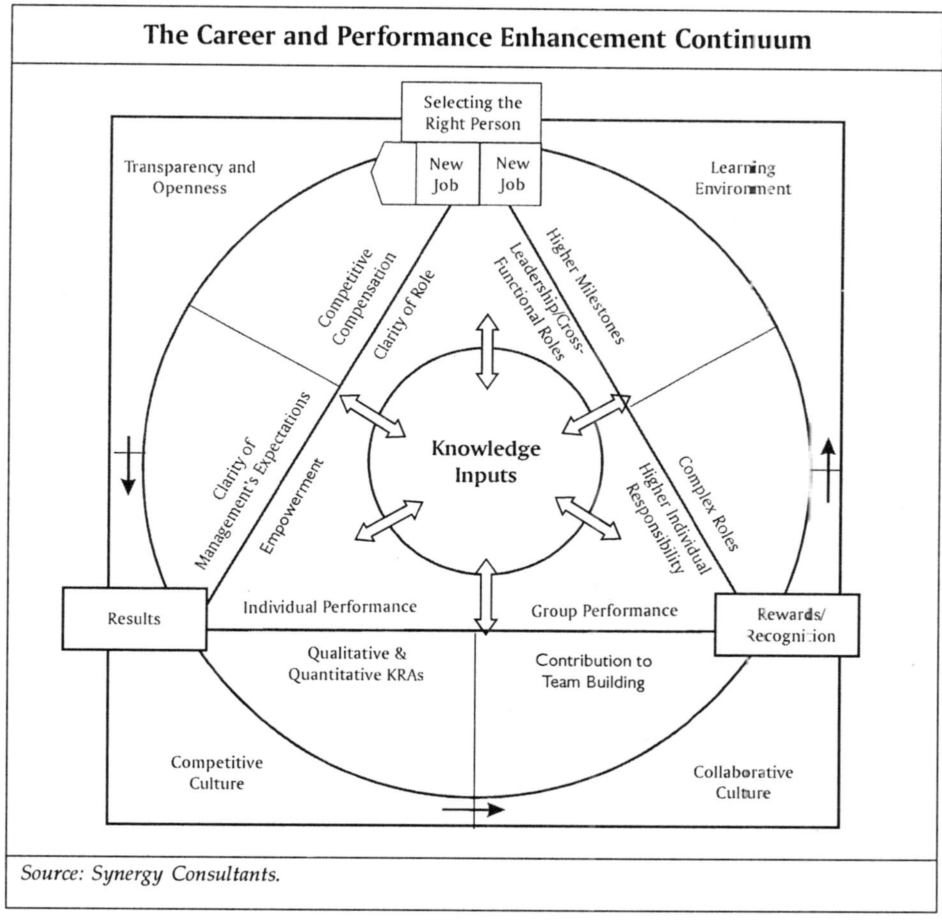

Source: Synergy Consultants.

The Rejuvenation Process

Knowledge is the primary resource around which the professional careers and performance revolve. The process of acquiring knowledge, strengthening and growing it with individual employees and groups, internalizing the learning, churning through the organizational dynamics to evolve strategies and initiatives revolve around people. Therefore, any disruptions and discontinuities in the teams affect the knowledge enhancement process and reflect on the bottomline.

The Career and Performance Enhancement Continuum is shown in the figure above as a simplified process.

The organization selects the right person, at the right compensation, defines and clarifies the role and the management's expectations, and empowers the individual. It provides transparent policies and an open culture that slowly grows into a competitive, collaborative and learning environment. It provides new and varied challenges and opportunities to meet and exceed the challenges. The employee excels in individual and group KRAs, contributes to teambuilding through mentoring. Rewarded and given greater individual responsibility, complex roles and higher milestones in leadership roles, he is again ready for a new job. A new job within the organization!

Re-recruitment is the key strategy of retention. Re-recruited in the organization with a radical shift and growth, the employee is recharged and propelled on a fresh journey through the Performance Enhancement Continuum. The process is repeated, adding exponential growth to the organization knowledge and performance curve.

The Future of People Processes

There is a marked change in the Indian economy with an unprecedented growth in the services and knowledge sectors. During the past year, my interaction with the HR and business leaders across many countries of the developed world has convinced me that this is just the beginning and like, say, the tip of the iceberg.

In the next phase of the growth, the knowledge industry would move up the value chain and more intellectually stimulating and challenging jobs will be outsourced to Indian companies.

The fact is that India is slowly emerging as a laboratory for incubation of knowledge, ideas and processes. In the years to come, the learning from Indian experience will be guiding businesses across the globe.

This has necessitated a new approach to HRM. It will no longer be a Human Resource Management issue, but of Human Resource Development. It will no longer be a role requiring training through standardized knowledge modules but of evolution and development of knowledge through providing and overcoming real challenges.

It will be a phase where organizations will focus on building strong knowledge equity. No one would like to lose this knowledge equity through attrition or disenchantment of its talented professionals. We feel talent acquisition and retention would continue to be a key driver of all HR initiatives in the knowledge economy.

(Gurdeep S Hora is managing director of Synergy HRD Consultants Pvt. Ltd., New Delhi, a leading executive search and management consulting organization in India. Today, he is recognized as an eminent management consultant in the area of talent acquisition, development and retention, performance enhancement, and developing solutions, HR systems and processes for greater efficiency and reliability. He can be reached at gshora@synergyindia.com).

9

Managing Career in Knowledge Society

Radha Mohan Chebolu

The growing 'career consciousness' among the youth to pursue a career-building strategy, while working in the organization, is found to be the reality today, and it demands an exclusive skill set for managing the 'learning' process as part of 'earning' mechanism. The success rate of career management by youth in contemporary times is decided by the ability of individuals in synthesizing their 'career passions' with 'professional obligations' for which both organization and employees have to draft their agenda with a missionary spirit. It is further testified that 'advanced learning' is not only aimed at providing a secured future to the aspirants but also strengthening the knowledge base of the organization.

Once upon a time, not too long ago, many employees stayed with a company or organization their entire career and at the end of it they received a gold watch as a gift, and some monetary emoluments packed with a praise note for their contribution and services. Employees often interpreted tangible signs of progress in workplace (moving from cubicle to office, changing titles) as signals that they were on the right path of progress in career. Even promotions were given very frequently as per the established norms without any extraordinary achievements by them. But the actual situation prevailing now stands contradictory to the old trends. It is observed that most of the people don't even know their career destinations, which results in a crisis situation emanating from loss of job. Lack of 'visionary outlook' and 'career consciousness' among the employees enables them to be the victims of the upheavals in business cycles.

Failure to withstand the evil effects of layoff strategies is also cited as one of the reasons for paying attention on building up a long-term career rather than short-term earnings. The 'contentment factor' is also driving most of the intelligent workers to pursue a career suitable to their knowledge levels. The concept of so-called 'job security' gets redefined in the light of changing paradigms of economy driven by global competition. The profile of industrial and service sector markets also get influenced by many factors leading to a drastic impact on workplaces. For more than a decade, unmindful of economic downturn, the combination of technological innovations and globalized markets have redrawn the business pursuits of many CEOs with an eye on catching the pulse of volatile situations resulting from competition and creativity. Even the public policymakers in government departments also started weighing their priorities in the management of human resources in public sector in the wake of emergence of market economy, and India and China stand afoot in the direction. It is not exaggeration to say that the 'workplace' has become 'work space' reflecting the nature of production and distribution channels that are emerging in corporate sector. Since the movement of goods is facilitated across the national boundaries, permeating the interplay of many market forces on the business profile of an organization, the employees have been the center of attention in making the organizations survive. At the same time, it posed a tough challenge to their skill sets and working mechanisms in the name of 'work pressure' resulting in mental stress.

The work pressure and stress are compelling the human resources of the organization to chart a new path for survival in the organization in the light of rising demands and changing priorities of the company. To stay or not to stay in the organization is not in the hands of the employer and is left to the 'conscience' and 'abilities' of the individual because his 'contribution' is the chief determinant rather than his 'competence'. Appearing as an indigestible fact, causing grave concern to most of the workers with traditional mindsets, a critical examination is required for identifying the underlying premise of this emerging situation. One possible reason for the growing 'job insecurity', which makes it imperative to pursue a 'career management' strategy in corporate sector, is the availability of plentiful options in goods and services for the consumers making them to rethink on their purchasing habits. These are the days the electronic tethers allow engineers in Bangalore to develop IT applications and interpret CT scans for American-based banks and hospitals; aeronautics specialists in Russia to design parts for the US aircraft manufacturers; and accountants in Manila to crunch numbers for the US corporate audits, says Shailaja Gaddam working with Oracle Corporation in Bangalore. She traces the 'novelty' and 'creativity' factors as responsible for the emerging situation. Name it as job insecurity or layoffs, resulting from the outsourcing of production and marketing, it demands a sound 'career consciousness' among the employees to stay fit in the organization, she further explores the situation. The successful pursuit of career graph, in the fast-changing world, requires a strong passion for 'learning', apart from satisfying the professional zeal for earnings by an employee, which depends on various pulls and pressures.

There is always a contradiction between employee's career perception and management's business line of thinking that needs to be resolved for enabling a smooth journey towards sustainable growth. The stimulation for employee performance as perceived by most of the management thinkers, in recent times, is not to be found with monetary packages. Instead, there is a growing concern towards satisfying career aspirations by potential knowledge workers for which, a congenial atmosphere needs to be created for an advantage of a win-win situation. The emphasis for career-oriented strategies by management, as part of business administration, is much wanted by the young generation that is coming up in India Inc. Mere association of a branded company with handsome package cannot guarantee the existence of an individual for a long-time career. Rather, it demands more commitment towards advancement of his skill set and knowledge levels in tune with changing dynamics of market economy, opines Ramavatharam Grandhi, Director, Pennidhi Associates, Hyderabad. With his acquaintance with corporate firms and their employees as a chartered accountant, spanning over a period of 17 years, he strongly refutes the argument that most of the youth are directionless and brings into light the growing 'career consciousness' among the knowledge workers. He identified a sea change in the youth's perception by saying that they are more inclined towards pursuing a long-term career, even in the backdrop of layoff by the company, by choosing an alternative source. Unmindful of job insecurity, they are much determined towards pursuit of their goals, which can be called a unique phenomenon in Indian society. The confidence levels of new generation are found to be much higher, according to his line of argument, when compared to old generation people who had the fear complex that made them stay back in single organization with many compromises and sacrifices. This argument brings into light the need for evolving a strategic perspective towards career by aspiring individuals and for which an attempt has been made here.

The visualization of emerging trends in the employment market makes us to draw a parallel between 'learning' and 'earning' streams of individual's career. As knowledge is infinite and knows no boundaries, the synthesis of earning objectives and learning goals has to be achieved as part of career management that alone can reward and award the human potentialities. As most of the Indian corporates are in the threshold of transformation mode, it is found to be an unfinished agenda and much needs to be done. The focus on promoting the career of employees is still in the infant stage as there are many bottlenecks on both the sides. But the initiative for management of career, without disturbing the normal job requirements, has to be based on the following parameters. As part of locating the impediments on the way to promote career of employees, this article underscores the need for achieving an organic synthesis between 'passion of learning' and 'profession of earning'. Though the pursuit of career management strategy is found to be individualistic and employee-centric, without the involvement of organization, the prospective employees expect certain initiatives from the management that facilitate career promotion according to their aptitude and abilities.

Time for Career Management

The necessity for toning up the abilities and skills required to stay fit in the competition are increasingly realized by the young generation. With a war spirit they are determined to fight the global competition resulting from 'outsourcing' and 'offshoring' trends. One needs to analyze the situation and accordingly plan the alternatives, while working in the organization, which requires rapt attention on market scenario. At a time when companies are looking for population growth that enhances demand, underdeveloped areas that ensure need for highly educated, cheap labor for cost-minimization and profitability, the potential aspirants for bright career have to update themselves in such a way that they will be the best marketable commodity. The management of career requires a close watch and analysis of market trends that makes them understand what sectors are growing and, accordingly, improve their skill set. This often requires the change of field and intrusion into other areas of knowledge as opined by most of the career specialists. With the increasing pace of specialization in various fields of administration, manufacturing and services, the need for advancement of existing skills and learning of new technologies becomes inevitable for the employees to stay fit in the competition. This naturally makes them locate new opportunities and their requirements as part of managing career on success path. By taking stock of skills he possesses at regular intervals, one attempts to update his résumé often with financial assistance from the company in which he works. Career aspirants should self-examine to show him where he fits not only in the organization but sometimes in the market also. What needs to be done to mould the personality, according to the demands and requirements, also becomes possible in this exercise. The visionary outlook makes one to look at the ads concerning the needs of the marketplace. When you look at 'help wanted' ads, don't look for job openings. Look for 'needs', says G Srinivasulu, Associate Director, R&D, Unit III in Dr. Reddy's Laboratories, Hyderabad. With his long experience of guiding so many young chemists in the beginning of their career, he observes that most of the people fail in making a career decision due to lack of proper awareness of their skill set. What are the strengths and weaknesses? Where they fit in the available options? These are the crucial questions one needs to put to oneself, says Srinivasulu.

The analysis of abilities and aptitudes becomes crucial as part of career management in knowledge-based industries, according to his observation. Even the time sense also plays a crucial role that enables a person to take a right decision at right time, opines Srinivasulu. He suggests that 'research career' after postgraduation definitely helps in promoting a long-term career and so the people who are working in R&D sector of IT and pharma need to have career perspective with an eye on future growth. The boom in opportunities is determined by the 'time' factor and so whoever rises to the occasion will be successful in his endeavor. Both for meeting internal competition and external pressures, one needs to be career conscious for which the learning process helps a lot. The passion for learning has to be made part and parcel of profession for which one needs to develop 'presence of mind' in the work. By having the presence of mind with a learning spirit, one can overcome the mechanical way of doing things. Viewed in this perspective, every day teaches a new lesson for the employees. Learning from experiences and observation is a kind of 'informal education' that leads to 'creativity' in job. One who excels in 'doing things differently' rather than 'doing different things' can sustain the market demands and chart a new career path suitable for him and the organization.

Career Contentment

As more attention is needed on the element of human 'psychology' that moulds individuals towards career path, we need to identify the impact of job profile on the satisfaction levels. It is often found that most of the skilled workers in knowledge-based industrial sector are not happy with the 'salary packs' and concerned about the nature and domain of the job they perform. If there is no scope for upward mobility and unearthing of skills and talents, they tend to develop the feeling of monotony, which, in the long run, drives them towards alternative career options suitable to their whims and fancies. Especially the up-and-coming programmers in software fields look for challenging assignments like 'software development' rather than customer support, says Syed Rajak, a California-based US software engineer. While recalling his past experiences during his stay with Cisco Inc., he emphasized on the element of 'contentment' that makes individuals to draft their destiny. As long as the IT professional is happy with the job given to him, there will be no measurable decline in output and quality. But the moment he finds the job boring and mechanical with no scope for application of brain and creativity, he tends to develop a kind of sickness which leads to deterioration in dedication standards. According to his analysis, this change in perception towards job also affects the quality of the project.

On the other hand, colorfulness of the job motivates people to find out alternative options leading to learning of advanced packages and tools. Therefore, the career graph of knowledge workers is always dependent on 'learning axis', which, in turn, is determined by contentment, says Rajak. Life shrinks or expands in proportion to one's courage and contentment traits, he further adds.

The job contentment also depends on the 'esteem' factor in some of the organizations. The organizations that are facilitative for promotion of employees' self-esteem are destined to mould the careers of individuals to the advantage of organizational interests. It further implies that the satisfaction of self-esteem makes people to develop their career within the company by balancing professional demands and inner passions. The flexibility in work schedules is found to be an instrument helpful for achieving this paradigm in career management. It is found that some people, lacking contentment in the job, pursue alternate career goals at the cost of job responsibilities leading to injustice to the organization. This is not a healthy trend as they are supposed to strike a balance between job commitments and career pursuits. It also implies that the effort to manage career goals should not lead to overlooking of organizational objectives and work culture.

Women as Career-Aspirants

The emerging trends towards break up of 'glass ceiling' in corporate sector stands as a classic example for the career pursuits among women in recent times. The increase of literacy rate in technical/professional education in the third world countries like India, proves the fact that the feel for independent career and earnings among women has been the order of the day.

Breaking the centuries-old clutches of bondage, a woman is becoming more assertive with regard to her rights and privileges on par with men that made her to pursue tedious working styles in corporate sector, exhorts Devaki Tadepalli, working as Head, Department of English in Montessori Mahila College, Vijayawada. She shares her feelings and experiences by projecting women's attitudes towards professional career as a historical necessity that alone provides a 'social security' in the current digitalized society. Balancing the homely responsibilities and professional obligations no doubt has become a Herculean task before them leading to unearthing of hidden qualities in women like patience, commitment and service bent of mind, she justifies.

More than 'financial independence', the level of 'social status' attached with careers in professions like law, management, finance and IT sector, in particular, is the motivating factor for youth, she says, while responding to the question on what promotes career consciousness in women. If we analyze the recent trends in the growing number of woman graduates leaving abroad for higher education and onsite assignments, it makes clear that the career orientation is found to be much higher in women when compared to men. It further endorses the above viewpoint. The reason for instilling confidence among women knowledge workers towards professional career is the expansion of job market and the growing need for dedicated personnel who could withstand the challenges and crises. The IT sector stands as witness for this phenomenon. The boom in ITES (Information Technology Enabled Services) and BPO sector moulded the careers of many girls who were considered to have mediocre talents. Their dedication towards career is testified with the night schedules in which they work. In addition to this, the growing competition from women in male-reserved sectors like transport, defense, etc., and in public sector boosted the morale of women towards dynamic fields. The corporates have to further probe into this gender aspect while enacting strategies for promoting the careers of employees as women are found to be more devoted and dedicated towards job. It is no exaggeration to say that the growing presence of women in both corporate and non-corporate firms is threatening the male prerogative making them alert and cultivating a competitive spirit.

'Employee Learning' as a Relocation Strategy

It is always debatable about what constitutes the management perspective in pushing forward the concept of 'Learning Management System' (LMS) in the organization. What tangible benefits the company can expect out of promoting learning skills among employees as part of human resources management? It is often observed that the employees can easily manage their education process, as part of building their careers, while working in the organization and it does not cost the management any additional expenditure and time. Compared to the unavoidable wastage in several organs of the organization, the expenditure of money and energies involved in employee learning management system makes no sense as it proved to be productive in the long run. The assessment of the performance of individuals during learning process makes the managers to identify the real cream and where they can fit into the organization. It enables the relocation of talents in appropriate places with focus on optimum utilization of human capital on which the management thinkers are concentrating.

Apart from generating interest in the job for employees the relocation strategy based on 'learning paradigm' triggers human passion for dedication and commitment. No doubt it's a tedious job, both for the management and employees, to pursue a career-oriented strategy with emphasis on further education and sophistication of knowledge, but results in long-term prospects. Sometimes the technology factor keeps the pace of this learning process alive. Thanks to information and communication technology boom that revolutionized the thought process by making the youth in India career-conscious and professional spirited. The faith that human capacities are unlimited and could be stretched in multidimensional ways inspired individuals towards career-oriented pursuits.

Performance Stimulant

Career planning has become a core area of attention in the management of human resources as it is expected to stimulate the performance of employees who want to expand their scope of activities. Mere confinement to regular responsibilities may not satisfy the career urge of dynamic personnel as described earlier. Hence, the provision for learning new technologies and improvement of qualifications makes sure a qualitative performance at the end. As such many schemes are being chalked out in the corporate and non-corporate firms for enabling the workforce to take part in career advancement. For example, in the field of 'academics' the prevailing 'Career Advancement Scheme' (CAS) is based on the premise of promoting the talent to higher grade with an objective assessment of improved qualifications and contribution towards field of study that is evident by the number of research 'publications'. Viewed from this angle, the learning pursuits by employees, as part of career advancement strategy, be it in academics or industry, result in stimulation of performance.

The more we learn, the more we act wisely, says R V Balaram, Import Assessment Officer, Inland Container Depot (ICD), Hyderabad. Considered to be a 'bureaucrat' with 'academic stint' he stands as a classic example for 'career management' philosophy applicable in the government sector. After getting selected in civil services examination to Customs Appraisal Service, he built his strong career while working in Ship Port (Visakhapatnam), Air Cargo in Hyderabad Airport with a bureaucratic instinct and won laurels for his position. After picking up valuable experience for more than a decade in the 'customs' department of finance ministry, he felt the need of upgrading his levels of exposure pertaining to economy that made him to pursue a PhD program in London School of Economics, London, by taking a study leave. He felt so excited and inspired to acquire a qualification in economics as he basically belongs to sociology department as a research scholar, before joining service. His career graph showing the achievement of highest degree from a world-class institution, while working in bureaucracy, makes it clear that 'career-consciousness' overcomes all hurdles of age, discipline and background. He strongly underscores the need, with his experience in balancing 'career' and 'profession', for 'capacity-building' as part of career management that can be possible through a passion for 'continuous learning'. He also suggests the need of developing good command over contemporary happenings, for all career aspirants, which can be possible through close acquaintance with print media.

People, who observed him from close quarters, say that he pursued the same method, which also helped him to develop a social bent of mind. Sky is the limit for learning, which instills the career passions in sensitive people, says another knowledge worker. So, growth in performance depends on the ability to pursue it cleverly. It is also found that constant learning supplements the intellectual capacities of employees in various ways. Harnessing the potentiality of employees, through career-oriented strategies, is much required for the productive benefits of the organization.

Multidisciplinary Learning

A study on the career consciousness, being developed by most of the knowledge workers, brings into picture the element of 'inter-disciplinary learning' catching the imagination of global managers in recent times. Since the IT field is open for many streams in engineering, non-engineering graduates in computer science and other traditional graduates with software exposure, it is found to be much difficult in managing the project teams with diverse backgrounds. As such, a need for 'project management' has arisen with focus on multidisciplinary learning.

For achieving uniformity and synthesis in idea implementation, people need to be trained on multidisciplinary lines with a strong zeal for efficiency and merit. It further implies that people who are conscious of charting out their career paths need to have a multidimensional approach in thinking that makes them to be comfortable in work schedules. More than the individuals, organizations are at an advantage if they give priority to interdisciplinary learning within the organization with a voluntary appeal. People who are interested in promoting their career can register themselves for these learning programs, which, in the long run, strengthen, the knowledge base of an organization. It further promotes a healthy interaction among diverse disciplines and departments leading to a congenial atmosphere in workplaces. The Satyam Computers is in the forefront by establishing an 'advanced center for learning' for the employees working in various branches. If handled properly, this kind of experiments save time and money and may prove to be beneficial to the organization.

Synthesis of 'Interests' and 'Priorities'

The above discussion on the need for promoting passion for learning among employees, as part of promoting their career, reminds us the need for achieving an organic synthesis between organization's interests and employee's career priorities. The service to the targets, set forth by the management, should not be at the cost of individual goals, Therefore, most of the US companies are in the task of redesigning the job profiles suitable to employees' abilities. As the corporate attention is focused more on 'time management', there needs to be a mechanism of 'Flexible Work Options' (FWOs), which can make the career aspirants to be at liberty for discharging their responsibilities. It gives ample freedom for creative people who can adjust their schedules accordingly. There is always a need to weed out the ambiguities and contradictions in management policies pertaining to organization and employee welfare. The mechanism for dialog process has to be institutionalized right from top to bottom. The bridging of gulf between expectations and performance of employees needs to be achieved. The identification of career priorities among the employees has to be undertaken through a process of consultation and dialog. The employee expectations of help from the management, pertaining to career, need to be discovered, which would clear the roadblocks and reward the merit. For achieving this synthesis in the organization, with a career perspective, the following steps are advisable for implementation.

Career Counseling Cells (CCC)

These are the days for career consultancies and planners and the organization's growth also depends on the ability to project its nature of inclination towards promoting the career of employees apart from achieving their business demands. Like in academics, every corporate organization too needs to have a counseling cell, which could rise to the occasion of meeting the employee needs and organization demands. Making them aware of 'growth options' and 'channels' within the organization, occupies the prime attention in counseling job, which, sometimes, makes them to stay with the organization. Lack of proper direction in work schedules and career ambition for most of the human resources, inevitably, makes them to lag behind. Sensitizing their duties and responsibilities needs to be done as part of promoting career, which alone generates bonds of loyalty between organization and individual. The darkness over the opportunities and options spread across the organization needs to be dispelled and the human minds need to be illuminated with clear-cut analysis of trends in trade. The focus should be on unfolding the hidden talents according to the requirements and that is what a sharp intellectual practice. The career counselors should embark upon the job of inspiring the workforce by drawing their attention towards emerging trends in various fields. Even the aspirants also should feel free to put forth their claims and objectives before the cell, which enables the management to understand the pulse of the organization.

Eyeing on Emerging Fields/Technologies: A Need for Career Diversification

The knowledge workers and skilled people, working in various domains of service sector, need to have a close watch on the emerging fields pertaining to their field of occupation. Especially in IT, the fast-changing technologies and platforms demand immediate placement of people with minimum exposure to the new technologies with exorbitant remuneration and sound packages. Most people fail in sensing the developments taking place in various domains due to their one-way application of brain to profession with no consciousness on market happenings. The pursuit of technology operations demands continuous watch on the field, which alone decides the path of diversification. Moreover, people who want to establish alternative careers must be watchful to the parallel streams nearer to their skill set and background. For example, the teaching community pertaining to the subject of English failed in grasping the emerging opportunities in corporate sector as language trainers in call centers, which are considered to be paying handsomely. Even people who study psychology, which is considered to be a dry subject with poor openings in the market, have potential demand as career counselors and soft skills trainers. They have relevance in the realm of 'personality development' that is demanding more attention from corporate managers. Diversification is found to be a valuable tool in the career management but with a good vision on learning paradigm.

Academic Interface

The much-talked-about interface with 'academics' is the need of the hour, for which, every corporate firm needs to identify ways and means. Developing bonds of interaction between 'theorists' and 'practitioners' is a welcome feature in corporate governance strategies. It is found to be a success formula in upgrading the quality of output also, as the people who work on various platforms of research in universities and laboratories will be at the disposal of corporate professionals. The scientist-manufacturer collaboration through MoUs, agreements would enable the industrial communities to establish new rapport with academics, which would promote their learning passion and zeal for advancement of knowledge. The corporate sponsorship of individual's research career and advanced studies deserve immediate attention as part of learning management, contends G Srinivasulu in his personal capacity. The sponsorships, though invite expenditure by the company, yield sizeable benefits to both university and industry. Acting as a bridge between academics and industry, the employee may turn out to be an asset at the end. The sponsorship programs help in brushing up the hidden talents and acquiring the needed skills. The Ford-MIT Alliance is the best example for corporate-academic collaboration leading to mutual benefit on both sides. Sometimes, undertaking a joint project, with a research lab situated in university, also facilitates a bright career for professionals and the technology is also permitting this trend. The University of Hyderabad has been successfully pursuing joint projects with most of the industries in IT, Biotechnology, Pharma sectors. The provision for external PhD programs by the university also stand as an example for this phenomenon of cooperation between industry and academics.

Roadblocks and Rewards

The way one perceives his own career, in the changing corporate scenario, decides his course of action by overcoming many roadblocks towards success. Most of the corporates are concerned about drawing the attention of workforce towards immediate gains rather than long-term objectives. The teams and groups, which are involved in delivering the goods on war footing, unmindful of sparing their own personal time, hardly find time to devote their attention towards their career. It is often found that the people who are placed in non-priority sectors of the company get ample time and energy to further their career pursuits. So, the management must make sure that all the human resources in the organization enjoy equal amount of work pressure, without giving place for soft corner and bias in work distribution. Sometimes, people who work hard get penalized with extra work and more number of stay hours which often goes unrewarded. This is found to be the most serious impediment, rather a roadblock, on the way towards progress in career. Hence, the recognition of the talented and laborious sections of workforce with rewards and awards may create working spirit and inspiration in the organization leading to acquisition of new skills by the career aspirants.

A long and promising career in the organization needs to be ensured for the potential workers who could willingly contribute to the growth of organization. When it becomes aware that there will be no upward mobility and enlargement of work, it causes job dissatisfaction affecting the quality of output. Hence, it is the lookout of management to create a sense of pride and confidence in their job, which makes them to develop a career perspective rather than discharging their duties mechanically. Relaxing norms and regulations, for the aspiring individuals to pursue their goals, needs to be done with a reform spirit.

Cultivating Competitive Spirit

By making sure, as described earlier, that the responsibility for staying within the organization lies with the employee in the changed environment for which the cultivation of competitive spirit is found to be mandatory. Acknowledging the fact that the competition sits not in the next cubicle but in other country, as evident from the outsourcing trends, one needs to have a realistic perception. The availability of cheap labor with more number of years of experiences in other countries drives the company to go for the the immigrant labor rather than relying on native workers. Hence, it becomes highly critical for the people to stay in the competition to demonstrate the value for the additional cost incurred on them through creative ideas, improved quality and expertise in management of work schedules with a lasting impact on organizational development.

What makes you unique? Putting a question like this tends to generate a competitive spirit and makes one to identify with the organization. Acquiring new technologies and knowledge relating to the field, with an eye on 'customer satisfaction', has to be achieved by the employee often without company's support. In the software industry this proposition stands valid as the career of a knowledge worker depends on the length and depth of his knowledge levels that makes him to be ever a learner. Constant updating of software packages, versions and operating systems alone could increase the marketability of cyber guys, says Rajak. The boom in technologies and tools enables people to catch up with the trends with a competitive spirit, for which one needs to have a close watch on market. The spirit of competition between companies should be relocated into the individuals as happened in the case of Oracle and Microsoft. Acquiring knowledge about the company's history, objectives, strengths and weaknesses, products and the supply chain makes one to be conversant with clients' attitudes, which guarantees his presence in the organization with a long-term career. One needs to be proficient in several languages to face global vendors and as such a cultural transformation is necessary.

Career vs. Family: An Inevitable Tussle

Any attempt to build a sound career on the foundations of integrity and dedication to the field of profession, necessarily, confronts with family interests as opined by most of the working people in corporate sector. Excluding a few areas like academics, government establishments and public sector undertakings, it happens to be a common phenomenon, in most of the professions, to have a confrontation between career demands and family obligations. Viewed to be a journey on sharp edge of a knife to strike a rational balance between 'work pressure' and 'family priorities' there needs to be better counseling on the family front. Most of the working couples, hailing from middle-class segment, had been paying heavy price to this rising phenomenon of devoting more time and attention to office assignments often at the cost of family time, say some young couples working in the IT sector.

The sky-high incomes and social glamor attached to corporate professions are motivating them to tilt towards career rather than taking care of children and family members. This attitude needs to be discouraged in the interest of preserving family ties intact, says M Shireesha, a sociology research scholar working on 'Changing Patterns of Family System in 21st Century'. She says, out of her personal observation and study, that the pattern of thinking in the young generation underwent a rapid transformation, which is found to be responsible for tilt towards career, unmindful of drastic consequences on the family front. She further exhorts that the cultivation of 'materialistic thinking' in the guise of 'consumerist culture' is driving the youth towards career promotion, often at the cost of family interests that needs to be addressed not only to preserve the value of Indian family system but also to prevent the future generation from getting trapped into 'nuclear family culture'. But, if we judge the ongoing trends in the market scenario, the growing priority of corporate workers towards professional objectives seem to be inevitable as it alone can equip them with the necessary vigor and vitality to face the competition. There is a growing realization among youth that the more they earn during initial days of career, the more they can enjoy at the fag end of their lives with no financial troubles. But the ignorance and insensitivity to emerging trends of 'communication gap' between wife and husband and other members in the family, in the light of ever-increasing 'career-consciousness', may prove to be disastrous in the long run. Somewhere, it has to be balanced and mere tilting of focus on one side could be harmful as seen in Western countries. But it all depends on the individual's conviction and has no connection with organization's involvement. The opinion that more number of hours spent on office can be compensated by devoting weekends to family, with all sorts of entertainment, seems to be another alternative to overcome this hurdle in career management.

The core analysis of factors that prompted organizations to develop a learning paradigm in their management strategies added with the steps needed to be taken for implementing the ideology is not sufficient to display the emerging scenario in Indian corporate sector. It has to be substantiated by the rising career consciousness among Indian youth that can be described from another dimension called 'practical thinking'. The growing levels of 'practical thinking' among youth also project a new dimension, known as 'entrepreneurship' that is gaining currency in career management strategies. Apart from satisfying the inner urge for 'self-dependence' and thrust for 'innovation', the youth entrepreneurship is also expected to act as catalyst in the ongoing synthesis between business priorities and employee welfare.

Practical Thinking Youth

It is widely identified as a strong determination, among the dynamic youth of today, to build a strong career in the chosen professions as it alone builds their economic fortunes with a healthy impact on next generation in the family. Apart from satisfying the 'urge for excellence', hidden in potential sections, the pursuit of a career management strategy is also expected to boost their 'purchasing power' as demanded by the rising index of cost of living. The women also grasp this kind of linkage between 'career management' and betterment of 'economic fortunes', which is motivating them to seek economic independence through a vigorous career strategy. It is not exaggeration to say that some of the progressive thinking women are taking up professions like law, medicine, chartered accountancy and the recent IT sector to escape from the clutches of 'dowry' problem that is still playing a predominant role in 21st century social system. According to a woman, with management background, working in software industry, the 'company tag' behind the name will boost up the chances of getting married to a prospective gentleman settled on a sound track. Being reluctant to disclose her identity, she further opines that there are certain instances where the working women are exempted from dowry demands. If not exemption, at least they could supplement the parents' pool of revenue with their sound earnings resulted from a sound career management strategy. As most of the working women belong to the salaried segment of middle-class in Indian society, who want to pursue the 'struggle for existence' through employment backed by higher education, the rising career-consciousness among youth has to be identified within a socio-economic context. The ground realities prevailed in business sector, as discussed earlier, further justify the visualization of career, by the 'gen-next', from a socioeconomic perspective. Call it by name 'maturity' or 'practical thinking' it deserves to be encouraged, says a veteran scholar from the management discipline with his long and chequered exposure towards Indian social dynamics.

'Entrepreneurship': As an Alternative Career

The practical thinking youth in the country are also endowed with a new 'culture', backed with growing levels of self-confidence helps them to develop 'entrepreneurship' as an alternate career in view of rising unemployment in knowledge sector. The growing cyber-unemployment is also causing concern to the potential aspirants, as there is much competition to available avenues. Since most of the companies and their HR professionals are unable to bring out any quality workforce from the pool leading to potential people left in the fray, there emerged a new thinking, among engineering graduates, towards entrepreneurship. As a result, they started applying their creative brains towards developing new software products, services and operating systems by floating individual concerns with a group management. We have many examples of success made by 'start-ups' in cyber world in the past when there was a boom for IBM Mainframe technologies. Falling in line, recently a young group of engineering graduates from an unbranded college named Scient Institute of Engineering and Technology, Hyderabad, have founded a small software company of their own, as there was no campus recruitment due to lack of brand image to the institution. Having applied their creative minds in their projects by making use of 'open source software' system, which is still in rare usage, they won 'award' and 'reward' also. These engineering graduates named Vamshi Krishna, Karthikeyan, Ratna Srikanth and Karthik Babu won the Red Hat Scholarship awarded by IIT Mumbai, Linux and Open Source Provider, Red Hat, and they are on their way to entrepreneurial fame at an young age. "We are entrepreneurs not job seekers", say the young graduates, who stand as live examples for those who want to pursue a sound career in corporate sector. The Rs.1 lakh cash prize, which they won for standing third among the project winners, has further helped them in their efforts to enhance Shishya, their 'e-learning' system that secured them the prize. The beauty of Open Source is that it allows you to download any source code and modify it according to your requirements, unlike closed source proprietary systems where you have to work with set software, says Karthikeyan. Having seen the beauty and charm among young entrepreneurs it becomes evident that the trait of 'self-dependence' and 'enterprising character' are found to be the essential features of career-aspirants that lead them towards success in their respective fields.

Conclusion

Since companies can no longer guarantee a long-term employment, career-tracks and pay increases, one needs to be conscious about his career, which depends on his ability to manage the learning process apart from eking out his livelihood. Preference for monetary aspects, while charting out new career path, needs to be done away if one wants a sustainable employment. Instead, the scope for learning while earning has to be identified which makes up the 'personality' of individual according to the trend. The achievement of a synthesis between 'learning' and 'earning' streams of an individual in the organization is considered to be a progressive step towards building a bright career. Mere lucrative offers from outside should not motivate them, unmindful of diminished work pattern and absence of vertical mobility, to quit the organization. How far the job assignment is going to strengthen the credentials and boost up the knowledge potential? What is the quality content? These are the questions one needs to put to oneself before devising strategies for career make-up. Mere qualification doesn't guarantee one's employability. It is only 'expertise' and 'in-demand skills' that are being taken care of by most of the corporates. "What have you done for me today?" is the corporate mantra today. Since most of the companies are struggling to respond to the global competition, this change in attitude is quite justified. Now it is time for learning while earning; though there seems to be a long way to go...

(Radha Mohan Chebolu, faculty member, Academic Wing, The ICFAI University. He contributes research articles in various business management magazines like HRM Review, Effective Executive *and* E-Business *published by the ICFAI University Press. His articles were published in* The Times of India, The New Indian Express, *and* The Hindu. *He can be reached at radhamohan@icfai.org).*

10

Virtual Teams in the Knowledge Society*

Sumati Reddy

The knowledge society has brought in its wake a large number of challenges and opportunities in the world of work. One major development is that individuals can now participate in different kinds of work without actually relocating to the place of work. This is possible mainly due to the advancements in Information and Communication Technologies (ICT). This article focuses on virtual teams and the associated challenges and opportunities for managers and entrepreneurs.

Virtual Teams (VTs) comprise one of the latest forms of work organization. Their development is mainly attributed to the growth in the usage of Information and Communication Technologies (ICT) for communicating and collaborating work across geographic boundaries and the advent of the knowledge society. This form of work organization allows dispersed talent and knowledge to be brought together and structured in a manner that allows VTs to achieve organizational goals. However, managing VTs requires the team leader/facilitator to be equipped with the right skills and knowledge to maintain team equilibrium and to exercise distance leadership. Issues, which may appear to be trivial in a traditional office environment, can get blown into serious conflicts in the virtual

* This article is based on the book *Virtual Teams: Concepts and Applications,* edited by Sumati Reddy and published by The ICFAI University Press; Pages: 232; Price: Rs.300. For more information and procuring this book visit www.icfaipress.org/books or write to serv@icfaipress.org

environment. This article highlights some of the challenges of managing VTs and also outlines a few opportunities offered by virtual teaming.

Challenges

Team Start-up

Management of VTs requires paying greater attention to the criterion of team formation. Membership in a team has to be balanced so that each member contributes to the overall effectiveness of the team. The social aspects of team development have to be given more precedence during the initial stages of team formation. Although all kinds of teams require paying attention to the social aspects of team development in the initial stages, it requires much more attention with respect to VTs. For this reason, face-to-face meetings play an important role in building social cohesion. Building such an interaction will set the tone for the spirit of teamwork during the subsequent stages of teamwork. Organizing a face-to-face start-up meeting, with the involvement of all the team members and key stakeholders of the organization, serves as an important upfront investment, which pays off during subsequent stages of the team's journey.

Team members have to be aligned to the team goal. Needless to say, it helps to have a compelling team purpose as it will enable the team to bind together. This meeting offers the opportunity to obtain clarity about stakeholder expectations, team membership, and roles and responsibilities of members.

It is equally important to make efforts to build rapport and relationship among members as this will determine team communication and performance. Members also need to build a communications protocol to ensure that members operate at a level which is clearly aligned with the team needs and competency levels of the team members. Hence, communication practices need to be instituted during the early stages of team formation.

While some of the recommended strategies may be common for VTs and conventional teams, VTs have to adopt a much more disciplined, proactive, explicit, and deliberate approach while addressing these aspects. Devoting adequate time and attention to these building blocks proves an invaluable upfront investment for starting up a VT.

Distance Leadership

Effective distance leadership in a VT context involves greater oversight of members' performance, motivation levels, and level of involvement with the team. These aspects can be gauged from the nature of interaction, work-related and otherwise, among team members. Issues which seem unimportant in the traditional office environment can be exacerbated in the virtual situation.

These difficulties affect team communications and the quality of team performance. There are five core categories of leadership skills aimed at addressing the commonly encountered issues among VTs. These skills center around the usage of communication tools which are appropriate for the situation, building of community, inspiring team members through clear and compelling goals, leading by example, and effective coordination. In addition to paying attention to these factors, VT leaders must consider the possibility of face-to-face interaction to supplement distance leadership efforts, whenever possible. This kind of interaction can play an important role in overcoming issues of social isolation, social bonding, and sensitivity to team diversity.

Communication

Communication among VT members takes center stage as the quality of communication affects the level of involvement and, hence performance. Different stages of team development and the degree of dependence among team members determine the style of communication to be adopted.

Leaders play a key role in directing the course and quality of communication as well as in instituting appropriate communication patterns among VTs. They have to pay special attention to team dynamics during the initial stages, equip teams with norms of communication and collaboration, and provide clear and ongoing support for keeping the team on track. They have to pay particular attention to nuances of communication, cultural values, and potential for conflict and misunderstandings. It has been found that overcommunication, in a virtual context, helps to avoid misunderstandings and conflict, and makes up for the absence of nonverbal cues in communication. Moreover, communication styles have to be adapted to suit the situation. These adaptations are determined by the stage of team formation, level of dependence on other members, and the cultural background of the team member. This includes a consideration of whether English is the primary language of communication by individual members. An awareness of the impact of different media, such as e-mail, audio, and video, contributes to greater effectiveness.

To enhance communication, care needs to be taken to avoid communication gaps, communication burnout, and boredom. There are several simple ways of avoiding communication gaps. It is important to acknowledge messages in various media—email, phone messages, voice mail, and fax—as this hardly takes any time. A message such as, 'Thank you for your message', not only avoids communication gaps but also helps in building a friendly group culture. Teams can make use of or develop customized systems to alert each other, ahead of time, if one is going to be away from the communications network for a day or two. This allows members to know what to expect. Communication burnout and boredom can be avoided by switching media for greater impact. For instance, if e-mail is the primary mode of communication, then the leader should make a telephone call on a regular basis, for instance, once a month, to establish a one-to-one communication with members. A short voice mail message also makes a lot of difference in enriching communication among members.

Human Resource Management (HRM)

Undoubtedly, the HR managers need to be prepared to face the challenges of facilitating virtual work by developing innovative ways to recruit, train, develop, and reward virtual workers. There are very few established norms or rules to guide HR managers in this endeavor. Since the organization of virtual work around VTs has been found to have the maximum success, there is currently a lot of emphasis laid on studying VTs and specific issues pertaining to their organization and management. The findings of such studies are important in guiding the formation of innovative approaches to manage virtual work. However, such studies are still in their nascent stages. One important issue, which is faced by HR managers, is the fact that they have to get accustomed to delivering traditional HR functions through the virtual mode. To equip themselves better, they have to familiarize themselves with e-recruitment, e-testing, e-learning, and the appropriate usage of ICT tools. These developments in HRM also imply that HR managers have to equip themselves with new skills and be prepared to respond to the requirements of speed and agility which are the characteristics of today's global business. Wipro Technologies has developed a program titled 'Meet Your People Program' which allows VT members to interact informally (Refer Box I).

Cross-Cultural Currents

Dealing with time differences, differences in communication styles, cultural misunderstandings, and lack of appropriate means to share knowledge, leads to the increased chances for interpersonal conflict among VT members. Different cultural contexts determine how members plan their time, diagnose problems, handle project details, commit to targets, perceive changes in schedules, etc. If cultural differences are not resolved in a timely and sensitive manner, it can lead to the erosion of trust. Sensitization of cultural issues, in a proactive manner, can help in effective communication, coordination, and planning. Team members have to be made aware of cultural aspects and must be encouraged to seek clarifications as and when required in order to avoid any misunderstandings. Building a social system with every project can be instrumental in meeting complex, cultural challenges in an interdisciplinary manner. Further, an atmosphere of open communication has to be promoted to ensure that culturally sensitive issues do not go out of hand. One must also remember that different media of communication have different verbal and nonverbal effects on

Box I: Wipro Technologies Enables Virtual Interaction Through its Online 'Meet Your People Program'

Wipro Technologies has a Meet Your People Program (MYPP), which is aimed at helping managers interact with their VTs on a regular basis. Apart from enabling the manager and the team members to share details pertaining to the project, the program also enables discussions regarding career, assimilates new members, and includes social events.

The company also has a 'war room', which is a virtual space where team members located at different physical locations collaborate in order to achieve a common goal. This enables members to collaborate on a real-time basis to discuss, coordinate and accomplish their individual yet interrelated activities related to the common team goal. War rooms facilitate document sharing, exchange of information, real-time online discussions among team members, sharing work plans, online updates to work plans and close monitoring of the progress of the team's activities. Access privileges and restrictions are critical for war room applications as sensitive information needs to be exchanged between team members who are privy to the same.

Source: "Best Practices of Managing Virtual Teams, Sudipta Dev", Express Computer, 2004.

misunderstandings, offense, and conflict. Face-to-face communication is the richest medium of communication as it is rich in verbal and nonverbal cues. Project management through global VTs needs to integrate cultural aspects into their management. This involves the consideration of the nine knowledge management areas of project management.

Opportunities

Several business opportunities can be capitalized upon by small and big companies alike as a result of the possibilities of interaction unleashed by virtual teaming. The list of opportunities includes joint ventures, strategic alliances, outsourcing, and customer and supplier relationship management. The opportunities are not limited to the business arena alone. They extend to fields such as education, healthcare, research and development, etc.

Business Process Outsourcing

One of the most significant developments linked to virtual teaming is the increase in business process outsourcing, which involves offshoring work to other countries where labor is much cheaper. Several organizations, at some point of their growth, need to consider offshoring core as well as non-core business activities to constrain costs and increase the speed of product/service delivery. They have two alternatives for doing so—setting up an offshore subsidiary and contracting VTs (third-party outsourcing). Both options have certain advantages and disadvantages. Since setting up an offshore subsidiary includes a lot of cost and time, outsourcing work proves to be highly beneficial in this regard. However, the final choice of the alternatives depends upon the requirements of the business and, hence, neither approach can be considered as the best practice model to suit all situations. The best approach for a business should be selected through a right blend of available models for offshoring.

Telecommuting and Teleworking

Telecommuting and teleworking are other examples of virtual work, which depend to a great extent on ICT to enable the distant workers to participate in the productive work. Organizations such as Aetna Insurance Co., IBM, Merrill Lynch, and American Management Systems, are just a few of the companies which are making full use of such opportunities to enhance their organization's performance. They have adopted innovative measures to encourage social interaction in the virtual mode to overcome the problems of social isolation that many

Box II: Telecommuter-Friendly Policies to Address Social Isolation

Maximizing 'Real Space' Interaction for Remote Workers

To counter the low levels of social satisfaction encountered by telecommuters, companies such as AT&T, Pacific Bell, Hewlett-Packard, IBM, Cisco Systems, Merrill Lynch, Arthur Andersen, Levi Strauss, PepsiCo., and Sears & Roebuck, have introduced telecommuter-freindly policies. As a result, the number of telecommuters have more than doubled, from 4 million in 1990 to well over 8 million by 2001. Some of the measures taken by these companies include:

- Requiring telecommuting employees to work in the office one or more days per week.
- Satellite offices: Employees work out of satellite offices nearer to their homes.
- 'Hotelling' arrangements: Employees can participate in 'hotelling' arrangements where telecommuters from several companies living in one geographic area share a part-time workspace that is available whenever they need the resources, social or otherwise, of a physical office space.
- Creating an active online 'community' for their telecommuting workers:
  - Aetna Insurance Co.: The company assigns a 'buddy' to each telecommuter to ensure that telecommuters have regular social interaction with other employees. This creates a social network, wherein, telecommuters develop social relationships with employees they would not otherwise have met.
  - IBM: Uses 'chat' technology to schedule social events for its online workers.
  - Arthur Andersen: Organizes informal chat room 'lunches' for its telecommuting employees.
  - Cisco: Telecommuters congregate in 'virtual cubes', which are chat rooms through which remote workers can communicate with co-workers whom they have never met or worked with. They usually visit these virtual cubes during lunch or other breaks. Similarly, Merrill Lynch uses the 'virtual water cooler'. These chat rooms provide the social benefits of a traditional office environment. Merrill Lynch has also made it mandatory for its managers to attend their company's telecommuting training programs, even if they only work in the office. This enables supervisors to anticipate and address the Internet-specific problems (social, technological, or otherwise) that telecommuters will encounter in the course of their employment.

Sources: 1. Xavier Reagan (2001), "Virtual Teams", Swimfish Inc.
2. Anne Tergesen, "Making Stay-at-Homes Feel Welcome," BusinessWeek (October 12, 1998), p.155.

telecommuters and teleworkers face as a result of lack of physical interaction with other workers. The efforts pertain to creative uses of ICT to bring telecommuters closer to other employees in the office, rewarding telecommuters for their contributions, and training managers to supervise employees online. Refer Box II for details on the measures adopted by some of these companies.

Virtual Universities

Virtual education and virtual universities are the latest developments on the horizon of virtual work. With global connectivity and deployment of sophisticated ICT tools, people in one corner of the world can easily communicate online with those in distant locations in other countries. Although education is a preoccupation involving a lot of face-to-face student-teacher interaction for a long period of time, usually years, all types of education are no longer being delivered in this mode. Virtual universities increase student access to valuable resources for learning, without the need to transplant from their hometowns to other locations. An example of a virtual university pertains to Universiti Tun Abdul Razak, Malaysia. When students learn to handle projects through the virtual mode, they become better prepared to manage virtual work in a business setting. A virtual educational platform offers them a safe platform to familiarize themselves with the nuances of virtual work.

Virtual Home Healthcare

Virtual teaming enables specialized and high-quality services to be delivered within people's homes. One such path-breaking development pertains to home healthcare of patients who need specialized treatment and who are unable to access specialists within their city or town. ICT helps in bringing together the patients, nurses, and medical providers on a common platform to deliver the much needed home healthcare. DITIS (Greek), which stands for Networked Collaboration for Home Healthcare—an Internet-based Group Collaboration System with secured fixed and mobile connectivity—is one such program that has been piloted and tested in Cyprus. It has been found to be very successful and is on the verge of being scaled up to commercial application. It has been developed by Barbara Pitsillides

[Association of Cancer Patients and Friends (PA.SY.KAF), Cyprus], Andreas Pitsillides, George Samaras (University of Cyprus) and Marla Nicolaou, Project Manager of DITIS.

(Sumati Reddy is faculty member and consulting editor at ICFAI Books, an affiliate of the ICFAI University, Hyderabad.)

11

Training and Development in Knowledge Society

K Mallikarjunan

For achieving results in the present scenario of technological revolution, effective management of IT is a* sine qua non *and it necessitates development of special skills in keeping pace with the technological progress that underlines the need for training and development of employees. All such training programs, in a knowledge society dominated by IT, should be directed towards the fullest exploitation of the unlimited opportunity provided by the ceaseless progress of technology. But the true spirit behind the programs in knowledge society should have every concern for providing good opportunities for training and self-development to employees with disabilities also.

A shrewd and successful optician was advising a fresh salesman he had recruited in his workplace: "Look, whenever a new customer approaches you and inquires about the cost of new lenses for his spectacles, begin the answer but don't immediately complete it. Just begin saying 'Rs.400 for replacement' and watch him. If there is no adverse reaction from him, complete your answer by saying 'for each of the glasses'. If there is an adverse reaction, complete your

Source: HRM Review, October, 2005.

answer by saying 'for both the glasses'. Your aim should be to sell at any event. Then only, I get my income and you get your salary". Despite its apparent frivolity, the joke does underline the need for training an employee for developing that kind of business diplomacy, which would ensure success in marketing deals with a customer.

Surely, it is only a trained employee who can deliver goods and help his employer/organization thrive. However, the concept of training and development is necessarily shaped from the viewpoint of the different stages of evolution taking place in the present-day world. The evolutionary process is witnessing the traditional structures like manual or labor-based activities, progressively yielding place to research and development and more sophisticated technologies. Also, those conventional knowledge systems that prevailed till the early part of the 20th century pertaining to scientific discoveries and inventions are giving place to more evolved systems. Information Technology (IT) has invaded every kind of operation from simple studies in the schools to complicated experiments by NASA, from simple shopkeepers having simple transactions to large engineering industrial empires. It is not, therefore, surprising that now almost all training programs include this subject and even schools include 'the system study' as a part of the early curriculum. The epoch-making advent of IT, and the prominence acquired by it in the life and business of the world community has brought about a decided slant towards IT in knowledge management functions and in related training programs for the welfare of the society.

Necessarily, the gamut and the depth of knowledge also undergo continuous expansion resulting in the need for proper knowledge management techniques. The attempts made to transform the traditional societal structures through 'knowledge management' results in the birth of 'knowledge society' and aims at attaining overall economic growth and prosperity. Charting out suitable plans for training and development, therefore, should be primarily aimed at developing the knowledge systems and channelizing them towards the welfare and progress of the economy.

'Knowledge is Power' may be a hackneyed saying, but it is a meaningful assertion. The statement highlights the vital need for basic intelligence and information for any organization or community—more particularly for the employees manning these organizations—to thrive in a competitive and ever-changing environment like the present-day world. The 'knowledge' and its management, being dynamic and reactive to the environmental change, call for thoughtful plans and adequate strategies accompanied by periodic reviews through properly trained key personnel handling the core activities.

The world community as a whole, with improving infrastructures, is thus becoming a closely knit web of the evolving knowledge systems that work in tandem towards the common societal interests and are rightly earning the cognomen, 'Knowledge Society.' In fact, because of the dominance and the indispensability of IT in generating, mobilizing, sharing and managing information through inconceivably speedy communication, this 'society' is turning out to be a 'knowledge and information society' and the need for trained personnel has never been felt more strongly than now. Simply put, the most distinguishing feature of a knowledge society would be its ability to collect, cull and interpret information, through properly trained personnel, and to use the same to the optimal extent for the benefit and improvement of the quality of life of the people, in general.

For keeping up the momentous transformation of refashioning, the societal structure, development of knowledge systems should take place at all levels, i.e., from the levels of governance down to the levels of communities, agencies and organizations. For achieving the desired results in the present scenario of technological progress, management and control of technology is a *sine qua non.* Since such measures necessitate development of special skills in keeping pace with the technological progress, the task of training and development is gaining increasing importance in every activity.

There is no denying the fact that, if any benefits accrue to society it would be through such technological progress and proper management thereof. A website www.totalkm.com/home.shtml devoted to the subject says: "To survive and succeed in the 21st century, communities and organizations have to be knowledge-based and knowledge-driven. They need to innovate on a continuous basis, share and socialize knowledge, and apply knowledge for their empowerment for greater effectiveness and for sustainable and equitable development. Knowledge management is the framework for synergizing the processes of knowledge production, sharing and application for maximum effectiveness and efficiency."

But the relevant question is:"How are these revolutionary developments sustained?" The desperate necessity for survival and the inevitable urge for a life of comfort for people, in general, are driving the world towards continuous evolution and change. Communities and agencies, committed individuals and societies, large commercial establishments, industrial organizations and commercial banks also, on account of their being the very foundation of the world economy in the globalized environment, have the onerous responsibility of making contribution to this evolution by adopting and applying the latest technological developments in their activities for the dual purposes of ensuring their own survival as well as discharging their social responsibilities. This contribution of the business world to improve people's quality of life is crucial in that it turns the spotlight on the subjects of employment and training personnel.

All organizations, whether corporates or banks or other establishments, are 'of the people, by the people, for the people', who need all encouragement as well as opportunities for honing their commercial skills to carry out this gigantic task of contributing to the general welfare. Hence, to be successful, skills acquired through properly planned training schemes and development plans at the organization levels are vital for the business establishments and commercial institutions. The well-known American author and consultant, Stephen R Covey, whose books cover many angles of the subject of human resources is reported to have said that "an empowered organization is one in which individuals have the knowledge, skill, desire, and opportunity to personally succeed in a way that leads to collective organizational success."

Of course, the approach and strategy for training of people will differ from industry to industry and from business to business. For instance, the contents and the duration of training programs for executives in a bank may be quite different from those imparted to the aeronautical engineers, or for that matter, to the people in charge of production in a drug manufacturing corporation. And within any corporation also, as the managerial activities widely differ, the program for each departmental group has to be oriented to the needs of that particular department. Further, the kind of training the supervisory or managerial staff require would also differ widely from that the hands-on workers require. According to human resources experts, despite the above variations, almost all programs do have a few common basic principles not excluding the orientation towards the all-pervading IT applications, the lifeline of knowledge society.

The common principles are:

- The program should be need-based from the viewpoints of the nature of work, the status of the trainee and the nature of the business and its goal.
- The program should further include opportunities for development of specialized skills and practices which would include all IT applications.
- It should provide, wherever required, practical demonstration and opportunities for hands-on experience, as also enlightening case studies.
- The program should unfailingly cover the legal implications of the 'dos' and the 'don'ts' of the industry.
- Social obligations like effluent treatments, preventive measures in cases of emergencies like fire, riot, and natural disasters should also find their places, wherever required.
- The governmental stipulations and statutory requirements like provisions of company law, tax laws, accounting obligations, etc., should invariably form an important part of the program, particularly to the managerial and decision-making levels.

Further, as the employee climbs the career ladder and reaches the level of senior management cadre and above, his functional horizon widens and his functions necessarily undergo considerable change. The contacts widen. Apart from acquiring knowledge and information about the industrial scenario, financial implications, business policies and marketing strategies, he faces a newer environment. The number of people that he has to handle both internally and externally increase. He, per force, develops a newer perspective of IT applications. He also needs leadership skills and the support of a larger team. These are the qualities that he would develop only through adequate training in team leadership building for managing the functions as the head of a skillful and effective team. He should also undergo a training process, wherein he would acquire emotional and psychological strengths as well as the ability to get rid of the negative emotions like phobias, complexes, and frustration.

Susan Hathfield, a management consultant in USA with specialization in human resources systems, issues and opportunities, says in her informative article available on website humanresources.about.com/od/trainingtransfer/a/training_work_3.htm: "provide training that is really relevant to the skill you want the employee to attain or the information he needs to expand his work horizons. You may need to design a session internally if nothing from training providers exactly meets your needs. Or, seek out providers who are willing to customize their offerings to match your specific needs. It is ineffective to ask an employee to attend a session on general communication when his immediate need is to learn how to provide feedback in a way that minimizes defensive behavior."

However, the very task of designing and imparting suitable training requires special skills for assessing the training needs and identifying the appropriate personnel for each kind of programs. Recognizing this vital need for training the personnel, especially from the IT angle in the knowledge society, many institutes have been set up in India for imparting training and skills for various cadres of employees ranging from employees of the government to the employees of public sector and private sector establishments. While the Central Government has set up some institutes like Sardar Patel Institute of Public Administration, Rajiv Gandhi National Institute of Youth Development, Indian Institute of Public Administration and Sardar Vallabhai Patel National Police Academy, the large industrial conglomerate, the Tata group of companies have set up Tata Institute of Management.

In this regard the website www.tmtctata.com/training prog_08_2005_Managing_training_n_career_devmt.htm devoted to this subject declares that the institute was started "on January 6, 1966. Its mandate was to serve as an educational institution which would assist, foster, cultivate and contribute to the development of professional management for the economic development of the country."

True to the above sentiment, Tata Institute of Management has organized many training programs in the past to executives drawn from various industries and professions. Since their own group is a large industrial empire having diverse ventures, the institute has been able to provide training for employees in hotel management, hospital administration and education management. The institute has also lent its facilities to various other all-India institutions like Indian Institutes of Management (IIM) at Ahmedabad and Kolkata, the Administrative Staff College of India (ASCI), Hyderabad, the All India Management Association (AIMA) and the Indian Society for Applied Behavioral Sciences. In fact, Tata Institute is believed to be playing a very important role in such vital areas like 'personality development' and 'corporate leadership', which are the needs of the hour. It is, thus, a veritable and exemplary contribution to the growth of the country's economy and to the society.

But the true spirit behind the training and development programs, especially in knowledge society, should have every concern for providing all the opportunities for training in skills and self-development to employees with disabilities also. Arguably, physical disability in any employee may not deprive him of the capacity to use IT except in acute cases of mental or psychic infirmities. If the mental faculties are intact, these unfortunate employees also could constitute good human resource in a knowledge society. History is replete with the anecdotes of individuals, stricken with gross disabilities, having brought about stunning achievements that are scarcely achievable by the ablest of men. Lord Nelson, the British Admiral and the exemplary hero of the Battle of Trafalgar was blind in one eye. Natalie Dutoit, the young swimmer from South Africa, won the silver medal in a swimming event in the Afro-Asian Games held in Hyderabad in 2003 in spite of her disability in one leg. Why not then provide every specialized program of training to the physically-handicapped employees, too, in the society that is knowledge-centric? It is certain, therefore, that given good opportunities and good training, these disabled employees would also rise to any occasion and would shine as assets for the employers.

In the US, the Department of Labor highlights the need for every support in training disabled employees and touches upon the positive outlook of strong-willed, disabled employees, who, despite their handicap, have all the aspirations and ambitions, as ardent as their able-bodied colleagues (Ref: www.dol.gov/odep/pubs/ek00/career.htm). To quote: "Employers must recognize that people with disabilities have aspirations and career goals. Supervisors should discuss career expectations with each employee, including an evaluation of the employee's interests, talents, and skills in relation to the requirements of available jobs. If an employee's career goals seem unachievable, the supervisor should provide constructive feedback and try to reach an agreement with the employee on appropriate goals and the path to achieving them. However, the supervisor should not assume that an employee's disability will be a barrier."

Undeniably, the training opportunities provided to the disabled require special attention and well-thought-out plans. Such thoughtful programs should invariably take care of the nature of the disability of the trainees. The disability may vary from visual impairments to hearing defects to handicapped limbs. Programs with the latest techniques like audios, visuals, etc., would largely serve the purpose. As long as the disability does not relate to the mental faculties, every disabled employee is as potential a human resource as his able-bodied colleagues. In fact, any employer, who identifies such physically handicapped potential human resource and taps it, would be making the most valuable contribution to the society as a whole.

All the thoughtful plans and comprehensive training programs would be down the drain if the trainee, whether disabled or not, does not have that inner urge, the motivation. He has to be motivated by igniting his inner urge. Hence, all the training techniques should be motivation centric, so that the trainee is able to bring out his best for the organization and thus to society. It is also a well-known fact that every employee, whether disabled or otherwise, feels highly motivated by the prospect of growth opportunities, performance recognition and decision-making status. As the motivated employee performs, it is the organization that reaps the yields. The public sector engineering giant, Bharat Heavy Electricals Ltd.(BHEL), which has been conferred the coveted status of *Navaratna* organization, has its own human resource development institute at Noida, under the guidance and supervision of Dr. Abbi, the executive director, with the avowed aim of developing its employees into skilled individuals and successful, result-oriented managers for the benefit of the organization.

The website www.lifepositive.com/mind/work/corporate-management/ Bhel.asp is quite informative as to how regular training schemes cannot only develop the employees but also benefit the organization: "The institute has massive training projects...Each employee has to undergo at least one week of training every year. At the Noida institute, senior employees are trained. The juniors are trained elsewhere," says Dr. Abbi. "We have a budget of Rs.60 cr and all R&D is done in-house...No wonder, BHEL has been conferred the status of a *Navaratna* (nine jewels) company by the Government of India. Last year BHEL won the prestigious Golden Peacock award, given to corporate training houses by Institute of Directors. Training programs include general management, behavioral sciences and functional management. For behavioral sciences, HRDI has specially trained some of its employees from the Institute of Human Behavior and Allied Sciences, Delhi. Our aim is to inculcate strong leadership qualities, because successful team leaders not only envision future goals and objectives but they also enlist the support of others in achieving them. Managers, particularly at the top level, get so engrossed in executing orders that they forget the other objectives... This particular program explains the prospects of future leaders, the difference between modern and traditional leaders, style of leadership, as also persuasion and politeness. Other aims are creativity, goal-setting, assertiveness, listening, motivation... Only when an individual is himself fully developed, he can transform the organization and make it successful."

Dr. Abbi opines that the need for training is more for senior managers: "As we steadily progress in the company, there is more need for a guiding force. Because with every promotion, the perspective widens; you meet more people and do more work. This training prepares them for the change. Once you are interacting more, you need to build your team skills. All managers aspire to become good team leaders; but few succeed. We inculcate values of trust, understanding, even try to get rid of fear, phobias and aggression. Sometimes, psychiatrists and psychotherapists are invited to help the participants."

The general management programs cover the economic and industrial scenario, business policy, marketing strategies, finance, organization and individual and group development. These programs have lectures, group discussions, case studies, films and the participants share experiences. The participants are also taught contract terminologies. Dr. K B Mehra, a PhD in business management, and additional general manager, BHEL, says: "Minor terms such as warranty and guarantee can have different meanings in legal language. We also hold training programs for other corporate houses. Sometimes our faculty is also invited to participate in seminars within and outside the country."

Further, this institute recognizes the importance of the emotional aspect involved in the training. Hence, Dr. Abbi claims that their training programs include yoga and meditation also. It is an example, where the East and the West meet in a knowledge society.

Finally, needless to say, all training and developmental programs, in a knowledge society dominated by IT, should be directed towards the fullest exploitation of the unlimited opportunity provided by the ceaseless progress of technology. While the trained employee acquires newer sheen, the organization acquires brighter bottom lines, the very lifelines of general economic prosperity that shine through the society.

Proper training does motivate many an employee to achieve excellence in his performance showing that if one 'acts rightly', i.e., if one subjects himself to proper training, he will achieve excellence. Can there be a more enlightening string of words than what the fourth century B.C. Greek philosopher, writer and logician, Aristotle, said?: "Excellence is an art won by training and habituation. We do not act rightly because we have virtue or excellence, but we rather have those because we have acted rightly."

(K Mallikarjunan is a journalist. He contributed articles to The Hindu Business Line, Deccan Chronicle, *and to the journals of the Institute of Chartered Financial Analysts of India, Hyderabad. His short stories have appeared in* Women's Era. *He also worked as assistant general manager in UCO Bank. He can be reached at mallikarjun33@rediffmail.com).*

References

1. www.lifepositive.com/mind/work/corporate-management/Bhel.asp
2. www.dol.gov/odep/pubs/ek00/career.htm
3. www.totalkm.com/home.shtml
4. www.tmtctata.com/training/prog_ 08_2005_Managing_training_n_career_devmt.htm
5. humanresources.about.com/od/trainingtransfer/a/training_work_3.htm

12

Knowledge Management
Why Learning from the Past is not Enough!

Rogério dePaula and Gerhard Fischer

Traditional knowledge management (KM) approaches aim to archive information from the past, so lessons will not be forgotten, implying that the information needs of the future are expected to be the same as they were in the past. The basic assumption underlying our approach is that knowledge is not a commodity to be consumed but is collaboratively designed and constructed, emphasizing innovation, continuous learning, and collaboration as important processes. Our approach to KM focuses on a design perspective in which workers as stakeholders create new knowledge as they carry out their work practices. Our goal is to enable innovative practices at a social level by supporting collaboration and communication. We see knowledge as an intrinsic aspect of collaborative design practices, in which stakeholders are integrating the knowledge they collaboratively construct into the (re)design of solutions and the practices themselves. Exploring this approach, our research has studied the design and deployment of a collaborative KM system, Web2gether, which was developed

to facilitate the creation and development of social networks among special education professionals. This effort has set the stage for a more systematic and thorough study of the integration of this technology into these professionals' day-to-day work practices. It has enhanced our understanding concerning the issues pertaining to the adoption of Web2gether as a KM system and its effectiveness in addressing its users' real information and support needs.

Introduction

The traditional approach for knowledge management (KM) often considers knowledge as a commodity (Murray, 2000). An alternative view of KM oriented toward design communities focuses on support for collaboration, communication, and development of social networks (SNs) among stakeholders in design activities.

A discussion on KM cannot be restricted to the epistemological analysis of knowledge or the technical evaluation of a KM system. It has to address the various scales of interaction that impact the work practices of those involved in the processes of introducing and employing new KM practices and systems. Although the underlying definition of knowledge, either as a commodity or as the outcome of a design practice, will influence the design approach for KM practices and systems (see Table 1), more thorough guidelines for design need to be complemented with a deeper understanding of social, technical, and organizational aspects of the context in which KM is to be employed. These aspects will help in unveiling the opportunities and challenges of the approach.

Toward this end, we have devised a more complete framework for KM based on the design perspective. In this framework, knowledge is regarded as being distributed among stakeholders and artifacts, being enacted while they carry out design activities within communities of practices and/or interests. As such, this framework draws on the concepts of distributed cognition, social networks, and information ecologies. A KM system to support this perspective should be based on the design of living organizational memories, which are evolving as collaborative repositories of information. This design approach draws on a process model for evolving and collaborative systems—namely, the seeding, evolutionary growth, reseeding model.

In this chapter, we describe and contrast the two conceptual foundations for KM to set the stage for an empirical study in which the design perspective was employed to support the complex and distributed work of special education professionals. This study has helped us further understand the opportunities and challenges in employing such a perspective in a real context. A successful integration of novel KM practices and systems into the work setting required major organizational and social changes, which can be facilitated or hindered by existing organizational structures (such as work, social, and incentive structures). Only through the balance between "the traditions and the transcendences" (Ehn, 1988) will KM approaches be able to respect these existing structures and at the same time help to enhance these practices with innovations.

The two perspectives outlined in Table 1 serve as the focus of the approach put forth later in this chapter. We start our discussion by describing and comparing the commodity perspective and the design perspective. Next, we describe our effort to apply the design perspective to a major project in which we created a collaborative KM system, Web2gether, to serve the needs of the special education

Table 1: Two Perspectives of KM (Fischer and Ostwald, 2001)

	Commodity Perspective	**Design Perspective**
Nature of Knowledge	Object	Enacted
Creation	Specialists	Stakeholders
Integration	Design time	Use time
Tasks	System-driven	User-driven
Learning	Transferred	Constructed
Dissemination	Broadcasting	On-demand
Technologies	Closed, static	Open, dynamic
Work Style	Standardized	Improvised
Social Structures	Top-down	Peer-to-peer
Work Structures	Hierarchical	CoP and CoI
Incentive Structures	Job assignments	Direct involvement
Breakdowns	Errors to be avoided	Opportunities

professionals for people with disabilities. Our research has shown the opportunities and pointed to some of the benefits in utilizing this system to support the work of these professionals. We focused on providing them with professional and personal support through the development of social networks. To this end, we designed Web2gether to support the distributed and situated work of special education professionals, by implementing the notion of social network in the core of the system. The design perspective is not without challenges. We discuss the lessons learned from our research and development effort, including some challenges in deploying Web2gether.

Two Perspectives on KM

In the traditional views of KM, knowledge is regarded as a commodity that needs to be captured, stored, and indexed to allow efficient retrievals in the future. The underlying assumption is that future needs are most likely to be the same as those of today. The responsibility for creating adequate "knowledge structures" to enable future retrievals from the shared repository of "knowledge objects" is delegated to specialists (e.g., knowledge engineers), who, at design time (when a KM system is designed and developed), create such structures.

Our work is grounded on a design perspective of KM that supports a design culture in which collaborating, working, learning, and creating knowledge are complementary aspects of the same social practice. From this perspective, knowledge does not reside inside one's head, but is distributed in a network of stakeholders and artifacts, and collaboratively constructed and enacted as work situations unfold. Stakeholders are reflective practitioners (Schön, 1983), who struggle to understand and solve ill defined problems. Learning is intrinsic to problem-solving because problems are not given but must be framed and solved as unique instances. Knowing in action provides a rich interpretive framework for individuals to cope with these new situations. As Schön put it, "our knowing is in our actions" (ibid, p.49).

This perspective has two essential aspects. First, stakeholders, not specialists, create knowledge. Knowledge is an intrinsic aspect of acting in practice and is created by those who own the problems as they emerge (Fischer, 1994). Second, knowledge is a collaborative by-product of work. By actively participating, stakeholders become "knowers," and by collaborating, they construct knowledge. These aspects are summarized in Table 1, which contrasts the traditional "commodity perspective" of KM with the "design perspective."

From our perspective, knowledge should not be treated as an object created, integrated, and stored by knowledge specialists at design time, to be later manipulated, transferred, and retrieved by users at use time (when the KM system is deployed and used), when they encounter problems and knowledge becomes necessary. It is instead one of the by-products of getting work accomplished, as enacted in collaborative practices by a network of stakeholders. In this network, these stakeholders, such as engineers, architects, government representatives, and local citizens, engage in the design of a joint solution to a common problem, and collaboratively construct the knowledge necessary to address the problem at hand.

Knowledge is integrated into potential solutions at use time by means of user-driven tasks, rather than being predefined at design time through a series of canonical (system-driven) tasks. In light of that, the design process considers learning as a process of knowledge construction acquired as stakeholders act and improvise, while carrying out their activities. In contrast, the commodity perspective regards learning as the transfer of knowledge from the "knowers" to the "learners." Knowledge is broadcast to an audience through standardized tasks, rather than being activated on demand.

These two perspectives emerge from and support two distinct organizational structures. Knowledge as a commodity rests on top-down social structures in which there is a clear distinction between those who create the knowledge and those who need and use it. From the design perspective, no clear line exists between these two groups in that those who own the problem and need the knowledge are the ones who help to create it and later integrate it into the solutions. The top-down structure often reflects the hierarchical structures of roles and power of work structures, whereas the peer-to-peer structure reflects the types of work structures that take place in communities of practice (CoPs) (Wenger, 1998) and communities of interest (CoIs) (Fischer, 2001).

Another relevant implication of a top-down approach pertains to the incentive structures required to maintain the ongoing processes of creating and integrating knowledge as practices differ from problem-solving. This approach thus fosters a discrepancy between who does the work and who benefits (Grudin, 1988). This requires formal reward systems in organizations to motivate the process, such as mandatory and/or paid job assignments. In contrast, in a bottom-up approach, the incentive structures are often inherent from the collaborative structures of CoP and CoI. Stakeholders in this approach are more likely to actively participate due to their direct involvement with, and ownership of, the problems at hand.

The design of a technology to support either perspective carries with it certain implications. The commodity perspective rests on the premise that knowledge will be acquired, indexed, and stored at design time to address problems at use time. This implies the design of a closed system, whereby information is preprocessed by knowledge engineers before the users of the system can make use of it. In contrast, the design perspective is grounded on the premise that knowledge is enacted in practice, and that stakeholders will activate the necessary other networks, information sources, and technologies, so they can address their situated needs.

Traditional Views of Knowledge

In the 1990s, a major strategic shift took place in organizations with the acceleration of the rate of political, economic, and technical changes as well as the increasing worldwide use of information and communication technologies. At the same time that such changes were paving the road for a global market, globalization reciprocally helped to accelerate them. The new tendencies of this "information economy" required organizations to shift from simply thinking about products and marketplaces to focusing on resources, human capacities, and core competencies. The ability to outperform the marketplace rested on continuous generation of human capital,"generation and synthesis of collective, and organizational knowledge" (Brown and Duguid, 1998, p.91). Particular attention was given to the challenges and opportunities of sharing and transferring knowledge within and across organizations. This became the major tenet and driving force of the traditional KM paradigm, which assumes that experiences lived in the past should not be forgotten in order to inform future experiences. Knowledge required and created thereof is deemed as a stock or resource to be captured, codified, archived, transferred, and disseminated, i.e., as currency. The major approaches to address the challenges posed by this view take a "taxonomic" (Tsoukas, 1996) perspective.

Such a perspective attempts to classify different "types of knowledge" in different organizations, which supposedly would create effective means for generating, sharing, and managing knowledge (Orlinkowski, 2002). Many classifications stem from, and elaborate on, the distinction made by Polanyi (Polanyi, 1966) between tacit knowledge and explicit knowledge. Other dichotomies associated with knowledge were thereafter elaborated, such as codified versus noncodified knowledge (Hansen, 2002); "know-how" versus "know-what" (Brown and Duguid, 1998); and procedural versus declarative knowledge. They represent important, yet limited attempts to explain how knowers know (or learn) what they know (or need to know) to accomplish their tasks.

Explicit knowledge is commonly portrayed as simply codified or codifiable knowledge. As such, knowledge is treated as information, or "know-what," which can be reified and thereby captured, codified, and archived for future reference, and often is removed from the context in which it was generated. In contrast, tacit knowledge is usually discussed as personal, non-articulated, experience-based, and skill-type bodily knowledge (Polanyi, 1966). It can be thought of as a latent ability, often acquired through experience that can be enacted and activated in the context of work practices. As such, tacit knowledge contains subjective elements that make it more difficult to articulate, and it embeds elements of a particular practice that makes it difficult to transfer from one practice to another, thus making it "sticky." It is distributed among stakeholders, artifacts, and the social environment, which together with norms, division of labor, and motives constitute the activities of a CoP or a CoI.

A purely taxonomic view of knowledge poses intractable difficulties to the design of KM systems. The articulation and (de)contextualization of tacit knowledge are widely debated, yet they did not solve problems. Due to the nature of tacit knowledge, namely being based on experiences derived from actions and interactions in a context, it emerges from a practice and cannot be always associated with a specific element that constitutes it. Because tacit and explicit knowledge are mutually constituted and thereby are *sui generis* (Brown and Duguid, 1998), the transferring of knowledge from one practice to another becomes inherently problematic. There is a need for KM researchers and practitioners to go beyond the dichotomies. Knowledge should instead be seen as the ability to enact knowledgeably in practice (Orlinkowski, 2002), as "know-how" integrated with "know-what" in practice, and as an emerging, often distributed, property of these practices.

These dichotomies have led to a narrow view of knowledge, organizational knowledge, and knowledge management. Knowledge has been regarded as a stock or a thing that somehow needs to become explicit so that it can be shared among stakeholders within and across organization boundaries. It fails to recognize that tacit and explicit knowledge are mutually constituted (Tsoukas, 1996) and cannot (and should not) be detangled from the practice from which they emerged. In particular, this view has led to two problematic notions of knowledge and the approaches to knowledge, namely, knowledge of the past and knowledge as commodity.

Knowledge of the Past

"Those who cannot remember the past are condemned to repeat it."

– George Santayana

The quote from George Santayana reflects the underlying assumptions pertaining to the traditional approaches for KM. The major goal is to archive "knowledge" from the past so that lessons will not be forgotten. This is a rather limiting view of KM because it implies that the information needs of the future will necessarily be the same as they were in the past. Subsequently, those who need information for the problem at hand are treated as simply passive consumers of information (Fischer, 2002).

Knowledge of the past represents an attempt to articulate knowledge gained from previous experiences in order to anticipate future problems and to inform future actions. In organizations, it takes the form of best practices, scenarios, technical and directive documents, and reports that are generated by specialists based on previous experiences as well as anticipated and interpreted future needs. The goal is to provide efficient ways for users to access and share such explicit knowledge, although it alone is most likely to be insufficient to help in solving the problem on hand. Two distinct problems thus arise from this view. One is the assumption that this static and somewhat limited notion of knowledge can the assumption that this static and somewhat limited notion of knowledge can handle the complex and dynamic nature of real-life problems. The other is that it relies on existing understandings of the work practices it intends to support (Orr, 1990) and on imaginative limits of those who create it (Snowden, 1998).

In analyzing the effectiveness of formal documents in supporting everyday practices, Orr (1990) asserts that directive documentations are "designed not to enable deduction but to direct technicians to the solution through a minimal decision tree" (p.171). The premise is that the most effective sequence of actions can be determined at design time by developers and knowledge engineers who have a strong understanding of the technologies they develop but are likely to have a limited understanding of the context wherein such technologies are used. Not only do they have to anticipate possible problems with the technology, possible diagnoses, and efficient paths to the solution, but they also assume that the problems technicians will face in the field and the instructions to solve them are context-free, due exclusively to technical mishaps. Orr shows the extent to which this approach alone has been elusive and ineffective. He argues instead that users' most important goal is not necessarily to "fix a machine," but rather the relationship between the clients and their machines, and their relationships with the clients—in other words, "to keep clients happy" (ibid, p.172).

Knowledge of the past is thus useful to the extent that it can anticipate future needs and be transferred across different contexts. It involves the articulation and organization of possible states and needs that can be anticipated at design time to address problems at use time. Hence, it constitutes a closed system. The "closedness" refers to the fact that the underlying sociotechnical structures of such systems are determined at design time and are unlikely to be modified at use time by the users. Closed systems do not give ownership to those who own the problem, but to a selected group of designers whose major challenge is to foresee all possible tasks and breakdowns in order to store answers to questions that might arise thereafter. These systems are likely to contain information that is chronically out of date and reflects an outsider's view of the work (Brown and Duguid, 2000).

Closed systems often limit the communication channels between those who own (or have mastered) the (sociotechnical) artifacts and those who own the their actions to those anticipated by a directive documentation (Orr, 1990), but their achievements and their innovative actions would unlikely be shared with other members of their work community via the "official channels." Innovation will likely happen outside the system. The sharing of innovations, "know-how," and successful work experiences—war stories—often takes unexpected pathways. Orr (Orr, 1996) revealed that, due to the absence of information or difficulties in interpreting the directives in the documentations, technicians expect to learn from one another, and, despite the individual character of their work, they make the effort to meet each other and to share their "war stories."

Knowledge as Commodity

> "Knowledge is presented as a commodity to be acquired, never as a human struggle to understand, to overcome falsity, to stumble towards the truth."
>
> – Postman, 1995, p.116

From an economic standpoint, the simple idea of being able to stock knowledge as a disembodied asset belonging to the organization was compelling enough for managers to open-heartedly embrace the KM vogue of the 1990s. From a technical perspective, the idea of manipulating knowledge as information was embraced as the solution for the challenges posed by the information economy in the information age. The emphasis on knowledge in organization has encouraged studies on the nature of knowledge that yielded the re-conceptualization of the firm as a dynamic knowledge-based activity system (Spender, 1996). The superficial and naïve implementation of KM approaches, resting on knowledge as a commodity, resulted in a blind emphasis on knowledge-based systems at the cost of de-emphasizing knowledge as an attribute of people (Brown and Duguid, 2000).

The commodity perspective reifies "knowledge as a stock or set of discrete elements" (Orlinkowski, 2002, p. 250). Studies based on the distinction between codified and noncodified knowledge (Hansen, 2002) exploit the underlying assumption that the major difficulty of transferring knowledge hinges on the difficulty of representing it. They show that the strength of the relations between knowledge seekers and knowledge providers affects the likelihood of "noncodified" knowledge being transferred. Although these studies have offered this important insight concerning the importance of social ties (both weak and strong) between insight concerning the importance of social ties (both weak and strong) between those who own the problem and those who have the knowledge, they failed to provide a richer account for the nature of knowledge. They basically treated knowledge as information.

The Fallacies of Traditional Knowledge Management

The traditional approaches for KM, which have mistaken knowledge for information and a commodity, can be costly. Brown and Duguid (2000) tell a story of a firm that spent a generous amount to takeover a rival, primarily in order to capture this firm's impressive intellectual capital, only to finally realize that its real competitive advantage had "lain in the operating knowledge of its line employees, all of whom had been let go" (p. 122).

Similarly, the somewhat blind notion that KM would allow firms to downsize their "expensive" staff by process reengineering, which has instead caused them to lose human capital and its collective knowledge that was instrumental for their operations. As John Thomas (Thomas, 2001) put it:

> It is a myth that we can simply "capture" the knowledge of a thirty-year expert in explicit form, so we can fire the expert and hire someone with no relevant skills off the street, who can now use the "knowledge base" to perform like an expert.

At the surface, it seems natural to use knowledge and information interchangeably, but there are significant social and technical implications in doing so. Information can be treated as a self-contained element that can be manipulated, stored, and retrieved, whereas knowledge entails a knower (Brown and Duguid, 2000) knowledgeably acting in practice (Orlinkowski, 2002). The focus shifts from studying only "what" people hold and share and the suitable technologies for doing so toward studying of the processes, whereby motivated actors become knowledgeable and share their "knowing how" in practice and the suitable social and technical contexts for doing so.

Simply designing so that experiences of the past will not be forgotten in the future is insufficient to adequately address the current (and future) challenges of our society. Such an approach emphasizes information needs, although the major challenge nowadays can be characterized as information overload. Designing for "anytime and anywhere" is not as relevant as designing to "say the right thing at the right time in the right way" (Fischer and Ostwald, 2002a). KM should be designed to support evolution and implement meta-design principles (Fischer and Scharff, 2000) to support a design culture.

Design Perspective: Social and Situated Views of KM

The greatest contribution of the Internet was not necessarily to facilitate reach (easy access to information) but to facilitate reciprocity (social exchange worldwide) (Brown and Duguid, 1998). Similarly, the design perspective for KM goes beyond reach to allow reciprocity. It recognizes the key role of human agency in knowledgeable performances (Orlinkowski, 2002), which are processes by which stakeholders are capable of knowledgeably acting in practices and thereby making appropriate and informed decisions concerning a problem at hand.

Knowledge is often portrayed as a possession that people carry around in their heads and transfer to each other, despite the fact that work is unlikely to be carried out in isolation, let alone without the aid of external artifacts. In contrast, we see knowing as mediated by artifacts situated, and often distributed, in the social environment (Salomon, 1993). Knowledge then becomes people's ability to act, participate, and make appropriate and informed decisions. Knowledge thus emerges from the synergy (rather than the synthesis) of distributed social networks of stakeholders and artifacts, operating in concert to help one another accomplish a common goal. It is no longer held or possessed, but fluid, distributed, and "activated." It focuses on the role of human agency in enabling the work to get accomplished in the context of a design practice within a CoP or CoI.

Due to the complex nature of social settings in which knowledge is enacted, it is critical to understand the various aspects that contribute to the formation of the sociotechnical conditions for stakeholders to accomplish their work, instead of focusing solely on the knowledge-transferring problem. To this end, we propose a conceptual framework to understand the sociotechnical conditions at design time as well as at use time. This framework attempts to guide the design of KM systems by highlighting the distributed and collaborative nature of design practices, and to help in the analyses of organizational issues that may facilitate or hinder the use of such systems. This framework draws on the following concepts:

- Communities of Practice and Interest: Design contexts in which the design perspective on KM emerges.
- Distributed Cognition: Knowledge distributed in the environment.
- Social Networks: Knowledge as a property of the interactions and relationships among stakeholders and artifacts.
- Information Ecologies: Complex, coordinated, dynamic, and dependable relationships among actors and information sources.
- Living Organizational Memories: Design rationale for the evolving KM system to support social networks.

Communities of Practice

The inherently social and situated nature of knowing invites us to consider a meaningful social structure in which knowledge is enacted, created, and shared among stakeholders. Such a structure should represent the social and historical contexts in which they are capable of acting, participating, and making appropriate and informed decisions. Social practice represents an important sociocultural structure that embraces most of these aspects. Through practice, members of a sociocultural community develop a shared understanding of what they do, how they do it, and how they are related to one another and to other communities and their practices.

Because individuals often work in collective settings, and knowledge is distributed among practitioners and their social environments, social practice was broadened to account for the relationships among these individuals within their working communities. Lave and Wenger (1991) define a CoP as a social structure that captures the interdependence and relationship among individuals, (legitimate) participation, communities, and sociocultural practices. A CoP creates the conditions for its members to exercise their ability to put their knowledge into practice (Wenger, 1998).

The ability to knowledgeably act in practice often is different from the "official knowledge" specified in manuals, directive documentations, and best practices. It emerges from experience and, more important, active participation in CoPs. For example, Orr (1996) shows that technicians must first learn about the work and the social settings, including the technology, in which, services occur so as to tackle the actual sources of the problems, which in most cases, are not necessarily technical. Such knowledge to act in practice can be acquired only through participation and experience, and mostly shared among members of the same community of practice.

Despite the informal aspect in most of organizations, CoPs are often very stable social structures. CoPs have histories, cultural identities, interdependences among members, and mechanisms for reproduction (Lave and Wenger, 1991). Such stability enables the development of trust, shared language, strong social ties, and common values, which facilitate the creation and dissemination of knowledge among the members of CoPs. Although CoPs are a powerful source of knowledge, they can easily be restricted by the limitations of their own worldview, that is, the risk of group-think.

Communities of Interest

Working on complex problems usually requires the collaboration and coordination of stakeholders from different CoPs. We define a CoI (Fischer, 2001) as a group of stakeholders brought together from different CoP, on the basis of a common concern or interest, to solve a particular complex design problem. They can be thought of as "communities-of-communities" that help CoPs to overcome the problems they create for themselves. In contrast to project teams, wherein employees are held together by a formal contract such as a business project, CoI stakeholders are held together by a shared interest. There are fundamental differences in their goals and motivations.

CoIs are often more temporary than CoPs and do not establish a social practice. They are characterized by a shared interest in the framing and resolution of a design problem and can be more innovative and more transforming than CoPs if they can leverage on the "symmetry of ignorance" (Rittel, 1984) as a source of collective creative innovations. Challenges facing CoIs are in building a shared understanding of the problem at hand, which often does not exist at the beginning but evolves incrementally and collaboratively. Members of CoIs must learn to communicate with and learn from each other (Engeström, 2001), although they may have different perspectives and perhaps different vocabularies for describing their ideas. Learning within CoIs is more complex and multi-faceted than legitimate peripheral participation (Lave and Wenger, 1991) in CoPs, which assumes that there is a single knowledge system within which newcomers move toward the center over time.

Because CoPs hold a single knowledge system, acting knowledgeably is often unproblematic and relatively easy compared to the challenges of operating within CoIs, which often do not share a common language and practice. Various social strategies have been proposed to mitigate these challenges and facilitate the sharing of knowledge and allowing knowledgeable performances within CoIs, such as: developing boundary objects (Bowker and Star, 2000), supporting knowledge brokers (Barbara and Clifton, 1992), fomenting the use of electronic communication systems, and disseminating "useful-practices" (in contrast to best-practices) (Orlinkowski, 2002). These strategies are important as attempts to circumvent the social and technical obstacles that often impede an effective exchange of information within CoIs.

Distributed Cognition

The design perspective requires a framework for studying the distributed nature of KM. Resting on a distributed and coordinated notion of knowledge, such a framework should account for the complex, distributed, and sociohistorical nature of human actions in the world. In our research, we have employed distributed cognition (Hollan, *et al.*, 2001, Salomon, 1993) as such a framework.

Distributed cognition holds that knowledge does not necessarily reside solely in a person's head, but is often created by and revealed in social practices, and mediated by sociotechnical artifacts situated in a social environment. One major contribution of this framework is to expand the unit of analysis for cognition from merely focusing on cognitive processes in an individual's head toward a systemic view of cognition delimited by functional relationships of the elements that participate in a task situated in a sociohistorical context. Another important contribution is to bring culture, context, and history back to the study of cognition. According to distributed cognition, all human activities are embedded in sociohistorical contexts, which are not solely created by local cultural and historical practices, but also co-created by each participant's own history and life-experience.

Social Networks

Social networks (SNs) offer a way to understand the complex dynamics of communities (Hillary, 1955), and how people exchange support, by shifting away from a sociogeographic structure toward a structure of interpersonal relationships (Wellman and Gulia, 1999). SNs help us understand how individuals share information, experiences, and support, and how they accomplish their tasks (Nardi, *et al.,* 2000). SNs are source of human capital (Coleman, 1988) that allow stakeholders to engage in socially meaningful collaborative activities, helping them recognize the importance of their cohort in the building of knowledge. The strength of interpersonal ties (weak or strong) is instrumental to community organization, the diffusion of influence, information and innovation, social cohesion, and emotional and professional support (Granovetter, 1973, Rogers, 1995).

The SN view of exclusively linking people needs to be extended to include information, resources, and artifacts. A knowledge-level perspective is required to extend the traditional view of an SN (Carley and Hill, 2001). Traditionally, an SN refers to "the who" in the organization, which refers to the active agents who possess the knowledge to get the work done. "The who" is capable of knowing some of "the what" or "who else to ask," and thereby capable of taking knowledgeable actions. "The what" is essentially information (i.e., resources, personal and professional support, and related personal experiences and stories) that is traditionally not an element of an SN. From the design perspective of KM, there is a need to integrate "the who" and "the what," and, more important, to support the synergy between them so as to allow knowledge to be enacted in practice. SNs in organizations thus become distributed cognition systems, the existence of which can be often attributed to balanced information ecologies.

Information Ecologies

The distribution of cognition in an SN creates the need for the orchestration of human actions to allow common goals to be achieved. Such orchestrated actions, as Hutchins describes in his account of ship navigation (Hutchins, 1993), can be achieved only through learning-by-doing-in-practice and, more important, through learning to become an active and responsible member of a CoP or CoI. The last construct of our framework concerns the nature of the relationships among all elements that participate in creating the contexts in which knowledgeable actors knowledgeably act. Its major focus is not on the synthesis of such elements, but on their synergy. Ecology can be thought of as a cognitive architecture—complex networks of stakeholders interacting, and thereby enabling information flow among them—and as a sociotechnical system.

The notion of ecology represents synergy among heterogeneous elements, and also alerts for the danger of ecological failure due to environmental imbalance (Nardi and O'Day, 1999). Ecology implies a focus on evolution, and the need to constantly nurture the relationships among its members. Hence, it should be given the time to grow, but not without its members' active efforts to direct and shape it so as to create adequate (social and technical) environments that, in turn, enable synergy among its elements. For instance, Nardi and O'Day (1999) describe the important, yet often unaccounted, work of librarians in corporate libraries. Librarians and clients often work together repeatedly and get to know each other.

This allows librarians to better understand their clients' actual information needs, allowing them to offer information that their clients would otherwise be unable to find. Conversely, clients know when and how to appropriately place their requests by knowing what to expect from the librarians.

As sociotechnical systems, these information ecologies cannot be completely understood by the study of its parts, but by the relationships among them, that is, the complexity of integrating technology into the environment as well as its use and its reciprocal impact on the practices and the technology itself. Such interrelationships highlight the importance of active participation of those whose work practices and everyday lives will be affected by the technology, the long-term co-evolution of activities and technologies, and the "keystone species"—individuals with skills, experiences, and motivations without which an ecological system cannot adequately function.

Living Organizational Memories for KM

Based on the message of this chapter that learning from the past is not enough, we need collaborative KM systems in which participants can go beyond the information given (Bruner, 1973) by creating new understandings and by learning from their peers. Informed participation (Brown, *et al.*, 1994), which transcends the simple access to existing information sources (Fischer and Ostwald, 2002b), requires social changes as well as new interactive systems that provide the opportunity and resources for social debate and discussion rather than merely delivering predigested information to participants. Systems that attempt to capture "all possible information" are closed systems, and they are most likely to fail in supporting all needs from real-world problems without being constantly reinvented.

To change KM systems from closed to living organizational memories (Terveen, *et al.,* 1995), we have developed a process model, the seeding, evolutionary growth, and reseeding (SER) model (Fischer, *et al.,* 2001) that supports the design and deployment of evolving and sustainable systems. The SER model describes three phases of evolution in terms of the stakeholders involved and their activities. The seeding phase creates the initial conditions for the adoption and initial use of a system. The evolutionary growth phase is characterized by a series of "creation, integration, and dissemination" cycles (Fischer and Ostwald, 2001), whereby relevant information that emerges from work activities is created, integrated, and disseminated by those who own the problem. Finally, reseeding is a stage wherein the system is reorganized to address future needs.

The SER model is supported, in turn, by meta-design. Meta-design is a design approach that attempts to create technologies that support content changes as well as structural changes at use time. It supports processes for creating new media and environments that allow users to act as designers. It enables structural changes at technical, social, and content levels, and it attempts to create a new mindset wherein users are no longer simply consumers of information, but are active co-designers (Fischer, 2002).

Web2gether: KM Support for Special Education

The Web2gether project is a multi-year-long effort embedded in the larger research project "CLever: Cognitive Levers—Helping People Help Themselves" (CLever, 2003) to understand and provide social and technical means for supporting the use of technologies in special education. Early in our investigation (Kintsch and DePaula, 2002), we found that one of the major barriers to the adequate use of technologies in this environment was the lack of professional as well as social support.

We then shifted our approach from simply offering a technical solution to facilitate the access to these educational resources toward a sociotechnical approach to offer means for participants to reach each other, and thereby create and develop SNs. Web2gether was designed aiming at this goal by helping caregivers not only find resources, but form SNs and share their experiences. Sharing experiences has been shown to be an effective design approach for KM systems in the context of distributed and complex work practices (Bobrow and Whalen, 2002). It aims to go beyond the mere access model of technology (Arias, *et al.*, 1999) by following the SER model. It is a collaborative KM system, which instantiates the conceptual framework presented in this chapter.

In our research, we were able to identify a series of conflicts and contradictions that emerged from special education practices, and opportunities to overcome some of these limitations with the support of the use of a collaborative KM system. The support for SNs is an important step toward the development of communities (of practice and interest). Our attempt to deploy and implement Web2gether in the schools has raised numerous concerns regarding its use and adoption. These concerns are presented here along with the lessons learned.

A Brief History of Web2gether

This project began when an assistive technology specialist from the BVSD created and distributed a CD-ROM with a large number of programs that were potentially beneficial for the education of students with special needs. The failure to see widespread use of the CD initiated our current research program and resulted in a conceptual framework for understanding the low adoption and the high abandonment rates of technologies in special education (Kintsch and DePaula, 2002).

To address this problem, the CD-ROM was improved with meta-data to support the location of the available educational resources suited for particular needs. This extension was still limiting to the extent that it could not support the "creation-integration-dissemination" cycles (Fischer and Ostwald, 2001) that are necessary to support adequate sharing of information among and across social practices.

Table 2: Development Phases of Web2gether

	CD-ROM	Web2gether	
Development	Phase 1	Phase 2	Phase 3
Data Structures	Categories	Meta-data	Personal experiences
Information Access	Browsing	Searching	Recommendation
Design Approach	Access	Access	Informed participation
Goal	Facilitate access to the resource by making them readily available	Facilitate the discovery of the resource by implementing searching mechanisms	Development of SN among caregivers to facilitate support to the use of technology in schools

We extended this approach by developing Web2gether. During the last few years, we have built a close relationship with the special education community, which has allowed us to collaborate on the design, development, and deployment of Web2gether. The information space of Web2gether was initially "seeded" with the software applications from the CD-ROM. This initial seed was considered to be a necessary condition to motivate users' active participation and thereby foster new contributions.

The system underwent three major design and development phases during this time. Table 2 shows the phases that have been implemented and assessed. It highlights the major design orientations in each phase, namely underlying data structures, major information access mechanisms, design approaches, and design goals. Aiming at providing support for the design perspective of KM and addressing some of the concerns from our fieldwork, Web2gether evolved to become a living organizational memory. The design focused on the following considerations (see Fig. 1 for more details on the implementation of this considerations):

- Ongoing support for the professional development process;
- Equal access to the professional development opportunities;
- Safe environment for sharing experiences and ideas in that participants have their privacy and confidentiality assured;

- Recognition and reward mechanisms for achievement and participation;
- Support for both institutional as well as individual requirements (i.e., a resource shared through the technology should address the particular needs of a student with disabilities and his or her particular educational goals based on the curriculum);
- Help for users to find others with similar interests, needs, and experiences, and to effectively enable them to find information/resources relevant to the task at hand; and
- Support for managing personal contact in order to facilitate communication and overcome the sense of isolation.

Web2gether allows users to share stories and personal experiences (Denning, 2001, Thomas, 2001) regarding unique cases in which users came up with effective solutions to address their unique needs. For example, in the Café (see Fig. 1) users may share experiences regarding unique behavior challenges in trying to facilitate inclusion of students in the general education classrooms; adaptations made on existing technologies for unusual situations not anticipated by technology designers (e.g., computer games originally designed for entertainment being utilized to help a student with severe cognitive disability to learn cause-and-effect concepts); and accommodations and modifications of curricular materials to meet the unique needs of students with multiple disabilities (see Area 5 in Fig. 1).

By making the accumulated experiences of individuals in an organization publicly available to each other, and in particular to newcomers, we hypothesized that Web2gether can help in establishing connections among weakly bonded individuals (see Areas 1, 2, and 6 in Fig. 1). Information sharing thereby facilitates the development of stronger social bonds among like-minded individuals facing similar experiences, thereby enabling the exchange of professional and personal support. Web2gether can enhance the practices in special education by helping these professionals connect with one another and get the support they need to cope with their day-today challenges (see Area 1 in Fig. 1).

The goal of Web2gether was not only to enable users to access information relevant to their problems at hand, but also to turn these resources into objects-to-think-with as well as objects-to-talk-about (i.e., to provide means

Figure 1: Web2gether Screenshot

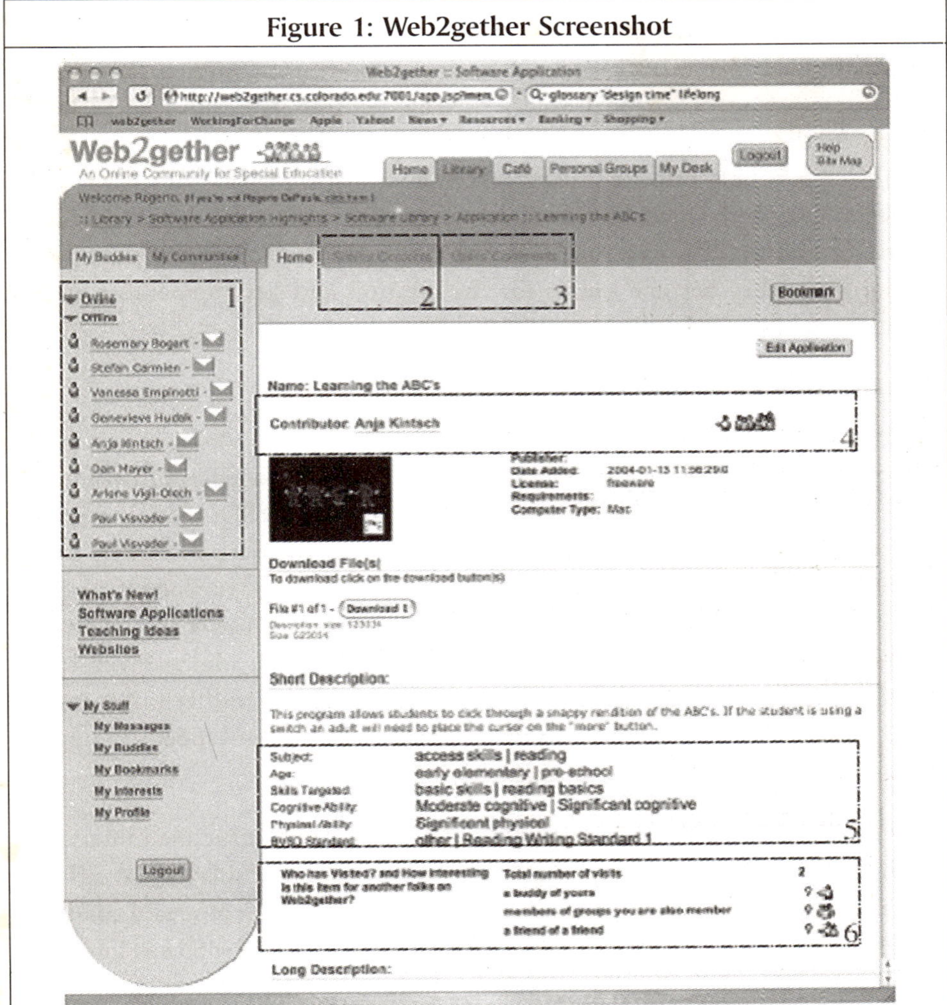

This figure highlights six major areas of the Web2gether system that address some of the design consideration presented in this chapter: 1) Management of personal contact information; 2) Support for finding resources relevant to the problem at hand (Similar Contents); 3) Collaboration and professional support (Users' Comments); 4) User's relationship with the contributor; 5) Support for institutional requirements and individual needs; and 6) Who is accessing?—social awareness based on social networks.

whereby users can interactively rethink their problems, reconceptualize information needs, and share their problems and ideas). For instance, in reading others' personal experiences and stories, a user could learn how to approach a given problem and identify unique modifications in existing technologies to support it. Web2gether makes use of stories as means for fostering the creation and dissemination of personal experiences by continuous learning to replenish and renew the existing stock of life experiences and educational resources. These experiences not only provide situated information regarding the context in which the technology and education materials were previously utilized, but also provide means for users to identify other users with similar experiences to ask for support. By doing so, they become means for the creation and development of an SN among those involved with special education.

Research Setting and Methods

The design, development, use, and assessment of Web2gether took place at various schools in the Boulder Valley School District (BVSD)—a school districted in Colorado, in which our research center is located. In the BVSD, special education services are available to all students whose disabilities interfere with their ability to receive reasonable benefit from general education instruction alone. Currently, the district offers special education support to more than 3,400 students, ranging from students with mild learning or emotional disabilities to students with severe multiple disabilities. Approximately, 165 special education teachers, 300 teacher aides, 15 occupational and physical therapists, and 30 speech language pathologists work with these students.

We collected data through participant observation, semi-structured interviews, and informal open-ended interviews. We conducted a series of site-visits at different schools in the BVSD, where we observed and followed the work of special education professionals, and we carried out a series of semi-structured and informal interviews with special education teachers and related service providers, namely occupational and physical therapists, speech language pathologists, social workers, and psychologists, to understand the issues pertaining to the use of technologies in the support of their students. We observed the work of several of these professionals working directly with students with disabilities, and participated in a few technology-training meetings.

Lessons Learned

Table 3 summarizes the lessons learned from our research. It highlights the major opportunities as well as challenges to the use of Web2gether by special education professionals in schools. Our fieldwork has revealed a great opportunity to apply the design perspective to support special education information and support needs. In contrast to the traditional views of education and classrooms, special education is a unique and complex work environment that involves not only the education of students with disabilities, but also continuous time, people, and resource management, not unlike a traditional office environment.

Opportunities for Web2gether

Special education teachers (hereinafter referred to as teachers) are frequently physically, professionally, and socially isolated from their peers and other professionals. Limited time for extra-curricular activities and the state of being constantly overworked (Barab, *et al.*, 2001) contribute to the lack of opportunities for sharing and for building relationships with other professionals. They have been unable to establish connections that would facilitate the sharing of "know-how," information, and support important to their day-to-day challenges in dealing with the unique needs of their students, namely universe-of-one. Experiences to help other teachers cope with emerging problems are seldom shared. Teachers often find themselves unable to deal with issues that peers may have already experienced and for which they found solutions. Not knowing "who to ask, and who to tell" (Kass and Stadnyk, 1992, Nardi, *et al.*, 2000) becomes a major problem in coping with the universe-of-one nature of special education.

Learning from the past may not fully address these issues. One example is the traditional teacher professional development method that hinges on training programs and the development of best practices or training is inadequate to provide the ongoing and long-lasting support necessary for a sustainable education of these professionals (Barab, *et al.*, 2001, Schlager, *et al.*, 2002). Being isolated and having to deal with very unique problems are great challenges in special education work practices, but they also offer great opportunities to the use of Web2gether.

Benefiting from existing information ecologies. Special education is a complex environment in which one finds a few cohesive information ecologies. Within these ecologies, information, support, activities, and technologies necessary for the adequate support of the needs of students with disabilities synergistically flow among special education professionals and through their artifacts and social practices.

Table 3: The Opportunities and Challenges of the Use of Web2gether

	Opportunities	Challenges
Nature of Knowledge	Universe-of-one	Highly situated in time and students' day-to-day needs
Creation	Teachers dealing with unique cases, create situated solutions to these problem	Time constraints, and motivating active participation
Integration	Matching solutions of unique cases with the problem at hand, and matching unique uses of technologies with the curriculum	Time and knowledge for doing the matches
Tasks	Find resources and support from others to help educate their students	Constant management of resources, and paperwork—impediments to the use of innovation
Learning	From each other's experiences and stories	Costs of actively participating and taking the time to learn
Dissemination	Reducing the costs by connecting individuals facing similar experiences	Time constraints, privacy, and lack of a culture of sharing
Technologies	Living OM and recommended system	Costs of learning to use innovations, acceptance of innovations and changes
Work Style	Constant needs for adaptations and modifications to match the educational needs and abilities of students—highly improvised	Overworked, and under constant time pressure
Social Structures	Overcoming the physical isolation or classroom limitations and constraints	Top-down (or institutionalized), lack of a sharing culture, and isolated
Work Structures	Reaching those facing similar challenges	Hierarchical, highly regulated
Incentive Structures	Personal initiatives	Difficulties to motivate risk-taking or learning
Breakdowns	Learning from experience, and improving existing practices	Lack of resources and time to cope with the costs of failures

They are, however, the exception rather than the rule—islands of success stories made possible by the dedication and hard work of individual persons. We saw an opportunity in Web2gether to provide a means whereby teachers can bridge these ecologies, find the professional and personal support they need, and share their experiences.

Important key species in these ecologies are the assistive technology specialists. They play a critical role in fostering the use of technology and the dissemination of information across schools. The use of technologies hinges on the active involvement and ability of these professionals not only to find the appropriate technologies, but also to collaborate with teachers and parents in accommodating, modifying, and learning how to use them. These specialists act as "knowledge brokers," bridging the gap between those who need support and the potential solutions. In realizing the role played by these professionals, a great deal of design effort was put on supporting their work. Not only are they likely to benefit the most from a broader adoption of Web2gether, but they experience a lower entrance cost (or threshold) to use it because their practices are more closely related to the use of such technology from the beginning. There is a higher value in using the system as well as motivating others to use it. In this regard, they play a critical role in disseminating the use of the system throughout the district because one important aspect of their work is to provide these professionals with new technologies.

Learning by sharing experiences. The exchange of stories is an important aspect of learning among special education professionals. They often share stories and life experiences as a means to give and receive technical, professional, and social support. Stories set the stage for discussions as well as create the necessary common ground for helping and learning to take place. They help these professionals learn from each other and understand the context in which solutions to the problems are employed, so they can attempt to carry them over to their specific situations and needs. We observed in our fieldwork that stories provide more situated and contextual information regarding the experience, allowing specialists to contrast the current situation with their previous experiences, and thereby come up with more effective solutions to the problem at hand. This is often the case among collocated professionals or those working in teams within schools, but it is seldom the reality across schools. The opportunities take place only in training sessions or in-services offered by the district. Web2gether attempts to help teachers overcome these physical barriers, allowing them to reach out to one another and exchange their experiences.

Much of the reality concerning the actual use of Web2gether was unveiled when we attempted to introduce it into the work practices. This has helped us further understand the barriers for change in the school environment, which hinders attempts to introduce Web2gether into its practices. We observed that these barriers for change became a major impediment in the adoption of the system. The usage and adoption of the system were directly affected as no changes in the existing practices and norms could be effected. We next describe some of these barriers when we introduced Web2gether into special education work environments. They highlight the major challenges special education professionals face in using the system to support their work practices (see Table 3).

Barriers for Change: Challenges in Introducing Web2gether

> "This book is not so much about stories to preserve organizations: it's about using stories to change them."
>
> – Denning, 2001, p xviii

Technological innovation is only one side of the solution for the challenges teachers face in their daily practices. For Web2gether to add any value to their practices, it needs to be meaningfully integrated into the overall organizational structures (i.e., social, work, and incentive structures). This requires changes in both technology and organization.

Changes are often subject to conflicts and resistances. The complex interrelation between technical and organizational changes is seldom reported in the KM literature. In our research, despite all the efforts to seed the information spaces with appropriate contents and despite the support from the department of special education in the district to facilitate the introduction of Web2gether into the classrooms, we faced many challenges to overcome the barriers to organizational changes.

Lack of incentive structures. The school system offers little incentive for promoting changes, taking risks, and adopting innovative ideas. The only reward for changing and trying to improve the education of their students is the teachers' personal satisfaction and the sense of self-fulfillment. Schools often do not reward their employees for achievements, but are likely to punish them for failures (Hodas, 1996). Teachers rarely take risks in implementing innovations whose benefits are not directly associated with the institutional interests.

Lack of time. Time pressure often hinders any attempt or willingness to find, learn, and use new technologies. Due to ongoing time pressures, teachers are more likely to see high costs in the use of a technology. They then face the dilemma of the active user (Carroll and Rosson, 1987): how to balance time to get the work done and to learn to use an innovation. The dilemma of the active user is related to the rational choices workers make while facing competing or conflicting situations, such as the trade-offs between dealing with pressing problems and investing in long-term solutions (such as learning to use a new technology). Overcoming this situation does not necessarily reside on learning outweighing work, or vice versa, but rather on the integration of both. Learning and working should become the same aspect of carrying out any activity in a work practice. Toward this end, innovations in the workplace have to be meaningfully integrated into practices, so that learning and use become the same activity through which users can see tangible benefits and long-term impact in their work practices and careers.

Tangible rewards and long-term investments. In normal situations, special education professionals are likely to take a more conservative position and carry out activities that are likely to have a clear and short-term impact on their work as well as their careers. For example, special education teachers are likely to spend a great deal of their time teaching their students to take the standardized tests because these tests have a direct and obvious impact on their work, as opposed to spending time engaging in activities to learn how to use Web2gether so that they can obtain support from other professionals. In this kind of situation, institutional pressures that clearly impact their careers eclipse any benefit from the long-term investments of using Web2gether.

Merging existing with new structures. In order to understand the challenges to change is critical to first understand the relationship between social and technical structures existing in the environment and the social and technical structures embedded in the design of a technology. The introduction of a technology often requires institutional and social changes to accommodate the new structures engendered in its use. If these new structures conflict with the existing ones in some respects, a barrier to change will ensue, and innovations likely will not be adopted. The reconciliation of these two structures can be facilitated by the use of participatory design activities as well as meta-design approaches to allow users to make appropriate modifications and accommodations in the structures embedded in the technology as the need for changes unfold through its design and use.

"Build it and no one Comes": Challenges in the Seeding Process

One major challenge in the design and deployment of Web2gether was that "we build it, and no one came" (Smith and Farquhar, 2000). Collaborative and evolving systems are of no value or use without users' active and informed participation and contributions. To help overcome this "cold-start" problem, the information space on Web2gether was initially seeded (Fischer, *et al.*, 2001) with the software applications from the CD. We hypothesized that this initial seed was argued to be a necessary condition to motivate teachers' active participation and thereby foster new contributions.

Despite the seeding process, no major use of Web2gether was observed early in the project. Ever during the design of Web2gether, we were not convinced that "if we build it, they would come."

Creating meaningful seeds is the first step toward this goal. The seed was originally regarded to be the technical infrastructures and the initial contents implemented on Web2gether. This notion had to be extended to include social infrastructures to support the use of the system in its users' everyday work activities. We concluded that a meaningful seed for a KM system necessarily has to address the existing information and support needs, but it should not be limited to technical functionalities and content. In our research it was fundamental to provide social infrastructures that permit users to integrate the innovations and changes promoted by the use the system into their everyday work practices.

A seed should be a bridge between existing practices (and the sociotechnical structures embedded in them) and the innovations (and the sociotechnical structures embedded in the design of the system):

- It should provide social structures that promote collaboration and connections between users;
- It should set the tone of the discussions and interactions to help them understand the possibilities offered by the system; and
- It should also be built on structured activities that help integrate the use of the system and their everyday activities, thereby facilitating its adoption.

A seed is a boundary object that, while helping users make sense of the sociotechnical system by linking innovation and existing practices, creates opportunities for them to rethink and improve these practices in this new context. It is the first step to facilitate a meaningful integration between "traditions and transcendences."

From Knowledge of the Past to Informed Participation

The "knowledge of the past" approach for the design of KM systems reinforces a passive notion of information sharing, in which users are supposed to act as consumers of information previously digested by content designers or knowledge engineers. It encourages forms of participation that are primarily motivated by an individual's interest in self-benefit ("what is there for me now?"), which is generally not conducive to a more sustainable participation, and thereby to the development of a living organizational memory. In contrast, the design perspective puts forth the notion of "knowledge as enacted in practice," emphasizing that knowledge is constantly evolving as a by-product of "knowers'" interactions with one another and acting in the context of their social practices. Knowledge requirements and workers' participations are not static—everyone is a potential knowledgeable contributor.

It is critical that users abandon a purely "consumer" mindset, and take on a more designer mindset (Fischer, 2002). This is a cultural change whereby users learn to take an active as well as informed role in the processes that directly impact their own work practices and social environments. Moving from the mere passive attitude of expecting to be able to access all possible resources toward a more active attitude of becoming informed participants represents a major cultural shift not only in the ways people make use of collaborative KM systems, but in the ways they do their work, interact with others, and see their roles in the society. It does not mean that users need to be active all the time, but to be willing to take risks, learn, and do things in ways that have not been imagined before in order to contribute to their personal development as well as the development of their social practices, and helping them to do the same. Only with this progressive attitude can collaborative KM systems such as Web2gether be of value to its users and to society in general.

Conclusion

In this chapter, we have proposed the design perspective of KM. It supports the concept of social networks in which communities of practices and interests work collaboratively and produces solutions to complex design problems. Knowledge is viewed as distributed and synergistically enacted by a network of actors when they carry out their design practices.

Special education is a complex environment that benefits from this KM perspective. Teachers face everyday unique challenges that require the expertise of a team of dedicated professionals working synergistically and collaboratively to help those with disabilities accomplish their daily tasks. In this environment, the knowledge of the past perspective is not enough.

Instead, our fieldwork has shown the opportunities and benefits in introducing a KM system based on the design perspective into special education as a means for continuous learning. We have designed and implemented Web2gether to help special education professionals obtain ongoing and sustainable professional and personal support and to have access to education resources they need to help their students with disabilities.

These benefits are not likely to be realized without the co-evolution of practices and technology. Technology alone will not solve the institutional and cultural challenges necessary for the implementation of the design perspective on KM. Major institutional and technical barriers for change need to be overcome. Changes will take place only if those involved in the design and development of innovations come to appreciate the delicate balance between existing cultural practices and innovations. Without a seamless integration of these two "worlds," we will not be able to create the necessary sociotechnical conditions for a new synergy between existing structures and new structures to emerge. Only through a careful balance between "tradition and the transcendence" will KM solutions be able to augment existing norms, values, and cultures with innovations.

Our research in this context supports the argument why learning from the past is not enough to help stakeholders accomplish their tasks practices. Knowledge is not a commodity to be consumed but is collaboratively designed and constructed in the doing of work. Our fieldwork has unveiled the opportunities as well as the challenges of implementing an alternative perspective for KM, the design perspective, which addresses this complex and situated nature of work. A complete discussion on KM cannot be limited to an epistemological analysis of knowledge or a technical evaluation of KM systems. It has to address the social, political, and technical issues of existing practices to guide the design as well as the introduction of KM innovations into the practices of those who will be directly affected by them.

(Rogério dePaula and Gerhard Fischer are with Center for LifeLong Learning & Design (L3D) http://www.cs.colorado.edu/~l3d Department of Computer Science and Institute of Cognitive Science University of Colorado, Boulder.)

Acknowledgments

The authors thank the members of the Center for LifeLong Learning & Design (L3D) at the University of Colorado, in particular the members of the CLever Project funded by the Coleman Institute, who have made major contributions to the conceptual framework described in this chapter. The research was supported in part by (1) the Coleman Institute, University of Colorado at Boulder; (2) the National Science Foundation, Grants (a) REC-0106976 "Social Creativity and Meta-Design in Lifelong Learning Communities," and (b) CCR-0204277 "A Social-Technical Approach to the Evolutionary Construction of Reusable Software Component Repositories"; and (3) SRA Key Technology Laboratory, Inc., Tokyo, Japan.

References

Arias, E. G., Eden, H., Fischer, G., Gorman, A. and Scharff, E. (1999). *Beyond Access: Informed Participation and Empowerment.* In C. Hoadley (Ed.), Proceedings of the Computer Supported Collaborative Learning (CSCL '99) Conference, Stanford, pp. 20-32.

Barab, S. A., Makinster, J. G., Moore, J. A., Cunningham, D. J. and Team, T. I. D. (2001). Designing and Building an On-line Community: The Struggle to Support Sociability in the Inquiry Learning Forum. *Educational Technology Research & Development* (ETR&D), 49 (4), pp. 71-96.

Barbara, D. and Clifton, C. (1992). *Information brokers: Sharing knowledge in a heterogeneous distributed system* (Techincal Report No. MITL-TR-31-92). Princeton, NJ: Matsushita Information Technology Laboratory.

Bobrow, D. G. and Whalen, J. (2002). Community Knowledge Sharing in Practice: The Eureka Story. *Journal of the Society for Organizational Learning,* 4 (2).

Bowker, G. C. and Star, S. L. (2000). *Sorting Things Out—Classification and Its Consequences.* Cambridge, MA: MIT Press.

Brown, J. S. and Duguid, P. (1998). Organizing Knowledge. *California Management Review,* 40 (3), pp. 90-111.

Brown, J. S. and Duguid, P. (2000). *The Social Life of Information.* Boston, MA: Harvard Business School Press.

Brown, J. S., Duguid, P. and Haviland, S. (1994). Toward Informed Participation: Six Scenarios in Search of Democracy in the Information Age. *The Aspen Institute Quarterly,* 6 (4), pp. 49-73.

Bruner, J. (1973). *Beyond the Information Given.* New York: W.W. Norton and Company.

Carley, K. M. and Hill, V. (2001). Structural Change and Learning within Organizations. In A. Lomi (Ed.), *Dynamics of Organizational Societies: Models,* Theories and Methods. Cambridge, MA: MIT Press/AAAI Press/Live Oak.

Carroll, J. M. and Rosson, M. B. (1987). Paradox of the Active User. In J. M. Carroll (Ed.), *Interfacing Thought: Cognitive Aspects of Human-Computer Interaction.* Cambridge, MA: The MIT Press, pp. 80-111.

CLever. (2003). *CLever: Cognitive Levers—Helping People Help Themselves,* at http://www.cs.colorado.edu/~l3d/clever

Coleman, J. S. (1988). Social Capital in the Creation of Human Capital. *American Journal of Sociology,* 94, pp. S95-S120.

Denning, S. (2001). *The Springboard: How Storytelling Ignites Action in Knowledge-Era Organizations.* Woburn, MA: Butterworth-Heinemann.

Ehn, P. (1988). *Work-Oriented Design of Computer Artifacts* (second ed.). Stockholm: Arbetslivscentrum.

Engeström, Y. (2001). Expansive Learning at Work: Toward an Activity Theoretical Reconceptualization. *Journal of Education and Work,* 14 (1), pp. 133-156.

Fischer, G. (1994). Putting the Owners of Problems in Charge with Domain-Oriented Design Environments. In D. Gilmore, R. Winder and F. Detienne (Eds.), *User-Centered Requirements for Software Engineering Environments.* Heidelberg: Springer Verlag, pp. 297-306.

Fischer, G. (2001). *Communities of Interest: Learning through the Interaction of Multiple Knowledge Systems.* In S. Bjornestad, R. Moe, A. Morch and A. Opdahl (Ed.), 24th Annual Information Systems Research Seminar In Scandinavia (IRIS'24), Ulvik, Norway, pp. 1-14.

Fischer, G. (2002). Beyond 'Couch Potatoes': From Consumers to Designers and Active Contributors. *FirstMonday: Peer-Reviewed Journal on the Internet,* 7 (12), at http://firstmonday.org/issues/issue7_12/fischer/.

Fischer, G., Grudin, J., McCall, R., Ostwald, J., Redmiles, D., Reeves, B. and Shipman, F. (2001). Seeding, Evolutionary Growth and Reseeding: The Incremental Development of Collaborative Design Environments. In G. M. Olson, T. W. Malone and J. B. Smith (Eds.), *Coordination Theory and Collaboration Technology.* Mahwah, NJ: Lawrence Erlbaum Associates, pp. 447-472.

Fischer, G. and Ostwald, J. (2001). Knowledge Management—Problems, Promises, Realities, and Challenges. *IEEE Intelligent Systems,* January/February 2001, pp. 60-72.

Fischer, G. and Ostwald, J. (2002a). *Seeding, Evolutionary Growth, and Reseeding: Enriching Participatory Design with Informed Participation.* In T. Binder, J. Gregory and I. Wagner (Ed.), Proceedings of the Participatory Design Conference (PDC'02), Malmö University, Sweden, pp.135-143.

Fischer, G. and Ostwald, J. (2002b). *Transcending the Information Given: Designing Learning Environments for Informed Participation.* In e. a. Kinshuk (Ed.), Proceedings of International Conference on Computers in Education (ICCE 2002), Auckland, New Zealand, pp. 378-381.

Fischer, G. and Scharff, E. (2000). *Meta-Design—Design for Designers.* In D. Boyarski and W. Kellogg (Ed.), 3rd International Conference on Designing Interactive Systems (DIS 2000), New York, pp. 396-405.

Granovetter, M. (1973). The Strength of Weak Ties. *American Journal of Sociology,* 78, pp.1360-1380.

Grudin, J. (1988). Why CSCW Applications Fail: Problems in the Design and Evaluation of Organizational Interfaces. In L. Suchman (Ed.), *Proceedings of ACM CSCW'88 Conference on Computer-Supported Cooperative Work.* New York: ACM, pp. 85-93.

Hansen, M. T. (2002). Knowledge Networks: Explaining Effective Knowledge Sharing in Multiunit Companies. *Organization Science,* 13 (3), pp. 232-248.

Hillary, G. A. (1955). Definitions of Community: Areas of Agreement. *Rural Society,* 20, pp. 111-122.

Hodas, S. (1996). Technology Refusal and the Organizational Culture of Schools. In R. Kling (Ed.), *Computerization and Controversy: Value Conflicts and Social Choices* (Second ed., Vol.). San Diego, CA: Academic Press, Inc.

Hollan, J., Hutchins, E. and Kirsch, D. (2001). Distributed Cognition: Toward a New Foundation for Human-Computer Interaction Research. In J. M. Carroll (Ed.), *Human-Computer Interaction in the New Millennium.* New York: ACM Press, pp. 75-94.

Hutchins, E. L. (1993). Learning to Navigate. In S. Chaiklin and J. Lave (Eds.), *Understanding Practice.* Cambridge, UK: Cambridge University Press, pp. 35-63.

Kass, R. and Stadnyk, I. (1992). Using User Models to Improve Organizational Communication. In *Proceedings of 3rd International Workshop on User Modeling* (UM'92). Dagstuhl, Germany: The German Research Center for Artificial Intelligence, pp. 135-147.

Kintsch, A. and DePaula, R. (2002). *A Framework for the Adoption and Abandonment of Assistive Technology.* In (Ed.), SWAAACK Conference, Breckenridge, CO.

Lave, J. and Wenger, E. (1991). *Situated Learning: Legitimate Peripheral Participation.* New York: Cambridge University Press.

Murray, P. (2000). Designing Busineess Benefits from Knowledge Management. In C. Despres and D. Chauvel (Eds.), *Knowledge Horizons: The Present and the Promise of Knowledge Management.* Boston, MA: Butterworth- Heinemann, pp. 171-194.

Nardi, B. A. and O'Day, V. L. (1999). *Information Ecologies: Using Technology with Heart* (First ed.). Cambridge, Massachusetts: The MIT Press.

Nardi, B. A., Whittaker, S. and Schwarz, H. (2000). It's Not What You Know, It's Who You Know: Work in the Information Age. *FirstMonday: Peer-reviewed Journal on the Internet,* 5 (5), at http://www.firstmonday.dk/issues/issue5_5/nardi/.

Orlinkowski, W. J. (2002). Knowing in Practice: Entacting a Collective Capability in Distributed Organizing. *Organization Science,* 13 (3), pp. 249-273.

Orr, J. (1990). Sharing Knowledge, Celebrating Identity: War Stories and Community Memory in a Service Culture. In D. S. Middleton and D. Edwards (Eds.), *Collective Remembering: Memory in Society.* Beverly Hills, CA: SAGE Publications, pp. 169-189.

Orr, J. (1996). *Talking about Machines—An Ethnography of a Modern Job.* Ithaca: ILR Press/ Cornell University Press.

Polanyi, M. (1966). *The Tacit Dimension.* Garden City, NY: Doubleday.

Postman, N. (1995). *The End of Education—Redefining the Value of School.* New York: Alfred A. Knopf.

Rittel, H. (1984). Second-Generation Design Methods. In N. Cross (Ed.), *Developments in Design Methodology.* New York: John Wiley & Sons, pp. 317- 327.

Rogers, E. M. (1995). *Diffusion of Innovations* (Fourth ed.). New York, NY: The Free Press of Glencoe.

Salomon, G. (Ed.). (1993). *Distributed Cognitions: Psychological and Educational Considerations.* Cambridge, United Kingdom: Cambridge University Press.

Schlager, M. S., Fusco, F. and Schank, P. (2002). Evolution of an On-line Education Community of Practices. In K. A. Renninger and W. Shumar (Eds.), *Building Virtual Communities: Learning and Change in Cyberspace.* Cambridge, MA: Cambridge University Press, pp. 129-158.

Schön, D. A. (1983). *The Reflective Practitioner: How Professionals Think in Action.* New York: Basic Books.

Smith, R. G. and Farquhar, A. (2000). The Road Ahead for Knowledge Management—An AI Perspective. *AI Magazine,* 21 (4), pp. 17-40.

Snowden, D. J. (1998). The Paradox of Story: Simplicity and Complexity in Strategy. *The Journal of Strategy & Scenario Planning* (Nov 1998), pp. 1-8.

Spender, J. C. (1996). Making Knowledge the Basis of a Dynamic Theory of the Firm. *Strategic Management Journal,* 17 (Winter Special Issue), pp. 45-62.

Terveen, L. G., Selfridge, P. G. and Long, M. D. (1995). Living Design Memory: Framework, Implementation, Lessons Learned. *Human-Computer Interaction,* 10 (1), pp. 1-37.

Thomas, J. (2001). *Information about Knowledge Management,* at http:// www.truthtable.com/know.html

Tsoukas, H. (1996). The Firm as a Distributed Knowledge System: A Constructionist Approach. *Strategic Management Journal,* 17 (Winter Special Issue), pp. 11-25.

Wellman, B. and Gulia, M. (1999). Net Surfers Don't Ride Alone: Virtual Community as Community. In B. Wellman (Ed.), *Networks in the Global Village.* Boulder, CO: Westview Press, pp. 331-367.

Wenger, E. (1998). *Communities of Practice—Learning, Meaning, and Identity.* Cambridge, UK: Cambridge University Press.

Section III

Cases

13

Knowledge Management at Tata Steel

*Ajay Kumar and Sanjib Dutta**

Tata Steel introduced a series of actions in knowledge management (KM) in its company in late 1990s. The company formed a 'knowledge repository', where all the employees shared their experiences and knowledge. Later, it formed 'knowledge communities' for like-minded people to meet and share their experiences. In 2001, Tata Steel developed a 'KM index' to assess the performance of individual employee in the KM initiative. Tata Steel was the only company in the world that was accredited as one of Asia's Most Admired Knowledge Enterprises (MAKE) during the year 2003.

* This case was written by Ajay Kumar, under the direction of Sanjib Dutta, ICFAI Center for Management Research (ICMR). It was compiled from published sources, and is intended to be used as a basis for class discussion rather than to illustrate either effective or ineffective handling of a management situation.

"We recognize and endorse the importance of knowledge as a source of innovation and competitive advantage. We wish to leverage all our associations within and outside the company to harness the ideas and provide the means for exchanging and growing knowledge."

– Tata Steel Annual Report, 2002-03.[1]

"I am proud that Tata Steel is recognized for its knowledge creating and sharing character and I congratulate all the employees of Tata Steel. This award, however, is only a milestone and must not be mistaken for our destination. We need to make knowledge the primary source of our distinction in an industry where technology is increasingly becoming a commodity."

– B. Muthuraman, managing director, Tata Steel, responding to the news of Tata Steel being named as one of Asia's Most Admired Knowledge Enterprises, in 2003.[2]

Asia's Most Admired Knowledge Enterprise

In 2003, Tata Steel was chosen as one of Asia's Most Admired Knowledge Enterprises (MAKE).[3] It was the only company in the manufacturing sector in India and the only steel company in the world to receive this award. The award was in specific recognition of Tata Steel's knowledge management (KM) initiatives, which were started in late 1990s. Tata Steel was the only manufacturing company in India to have implemented KM. Tata Steel's management expected KM to play a key role in establishing intellectual assets, rather than physical assets, as the growth driver of the company. KM was also expected to be an important source of competitive advantage for Tata Steel.

Tata Steel was early to recognize the significance of KM for the success of a company. It made it compulsory for all its employees to participate actively in its KM program. The company based its new performance assessment program on the participation of each individual employee in the KM program through the introduction of a "KM index."[4] The index tallied the points achieved through participation in the KM program, giving the employees a benchmark for their participation. Tata Steel also encouraged employees to experiment with new ideas, for which they were rewarded.

Tata Steel's KM initiatives were successful and the number of hits at KM sites of Tata Steel in 2001-02 was 1,100 compared to Shell's (second most admired company in Europe) 1,000 hits, even though Tata Steel had only 3,000 registered users as compared to Shell's 10,000 registered users. Through Tata Steel's KM initiatives, expert skills became available throughout the organization and productivity increased. As employees were encouraged to come out with innovative ideas, their job satisfaction increased, and another benefit was a reduction in the R&D expenditure.

Background Note

Tata Steel was established in 1907 by J N Tata[5] at Jamshedpur in Bihar, India. The company commenced production in 1911 with a capacity of 0.1 million tonne of mild steel.[6] By 1958, its capacity had increased to 2 million tonnes. Over the years, Tata Steel acquired several companies. In 1973, it took over some flux mines and collieries near Jharia, West Bokaro.[7] In 1983, it acquired the Indian Tube Co. Ltd., a manufacturer of seamless and welded tubes. In 1991, it acquired the ferro-chrome unit of OMC Alloys Ltd., near Bamnipal in Orissa.

Today, Tata Steel produces a wide range of products (refer Exhibit I) including hot rolled/cold rolled (HR/CR) coils[8] and sheets, tubes, construction bars, forging quality steel, rods, structurals, strips and bearings. It also manufactures material handling equipment, ferro alloys and other minerals, provides software for process controls, and also provides cargo-handling services.

In the early 1980s, the company initiated a modernization program for its steel plants (refer Exhibit II). Explaining the need for modernization, J J Irani, the then managing director of Tata Steel said, "We would have been finished otherwise ... you cannot fight a modern-day war with weapons of the Mahabharata. We would have been annihilated had we not modernized. We realized this and embarked on the four phases of modernization. We addressed our drawbacks like the steel making process, our weakest link."[9]

By the mid-1990s, Tata Steel was Asia's first and India's largest integrated steel producer (ISP)[10] in the private sector. By 2000, eight divisions of Tata Steel had been ISO-14001[11] certified; the divisions were the Noamundi Iron Operations, West Bokaro Collieries, Ferro Alloy Plant, Joda, Sukinda Chromite Mines, Joda

Exhibit I: Tata Steel Product Categories

Product Categories	Products
Agrico	Powrahs & mamooties (hoes), crowbars, kudalies (pick axe) beaters & mattocks, shovels, hammers
Automation	Under this category, company offered automation products to various industries
Bearings	Deep grove ball bearings, double row self-aligning ball bearings, magneto bearings, clutch release bearings, tapered roller bearing
Ferro alloys & minerals	Chrome ore, chrome concentrate, iron ore, manganese ore
Flat products	Hot rolled products—ex-mill (coil), ex-shearing Line (sheets & plates), ex-service centres, Cr products Galvanized products—galvanised plain spangled, galvanised plain with differential coating, galvanised Plain zero spangle, galvanised plain skin passed, Galvannealed, galvanised corrugated gc sheet
Long products	Billets – (wrm, mm); ingots – bar mill
Rings	High speed forming line, wagner 400 ring rolling line, radial axial rolling line
Secondary products	Remelting scrap, rerolling scrap, non-ferrous scrap, tubes-scrap, hr/cr scrap, by-products from collieries, Coke fractions, lime fractions, granulated slag, coaltar
Tubes	Standard tubes, precision tubes, closed structurals, welded line pipes

Source: www.tatasteel.com

East Iron Mines, Tubes Division, and Growth Shop & Steel Works. By early 2000, Tata Steel had completed four phases of its modernization program with an investment of about Rs.60 billion.[12] The company spent Rs.4 billion on consultancy fee between 1990 and 2000. The fifth phase of the program commenced in April 2000. This phase focused on attracting, developing and retaining the company's most valuable asset, its people, under its Performance Ethic Program (refer Exhibit III). In April 2000, Tata Steel commissioned its Cold Rolling Mill (CRM) plant at Jamshedpur. Together with its operational excellence drive, Tata Steel also focused on garnering more market share and on increasing revenues.

Figure I: Knowledge System

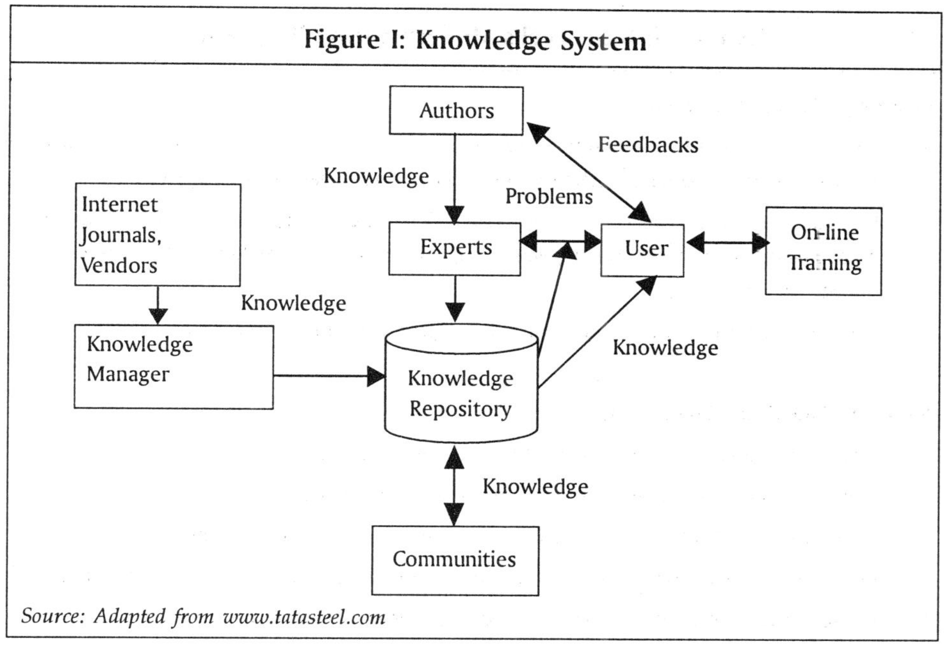

Source: Adapted from www.tatasteel.com

By April 2001, Tata Steel was the world's lowest-cost producer of steel. Tata Steel's operating cost at the 'hot metal' (liquid) stage was $75 per tonne. The company's cost per tonne of finished steel stood at $152, for the financial year ending March 2001. World Steel Dynamics (WSD)[13] identified and ranked 12 companies as World Class Steel Makers. In this ranking, Tata Steel stood at number one with a score of 131 points, ahead of Usinor (France), and Posco (South Korea).

In August 2001, B. Muthuraman (Muthuraman) took over as managing director of Tata Steel. He stepped up efforts to increase the profitability of the company. In late 2001, he announced a new program known as Vision 2007, aimed at making Tata Steel's Economic Value Added (EVA) positive[14] by the year 2007. Within a year of the launch of Vision 2007, Tata Steel became EVA positive.

In 2003, Tata Steel declared a turnover of Rs.98.44 billion with profit after tax of Rs.10.12 billion; it was the most profitable steel company in India. The company's success was attributed to its focus on operational excellence and its branding initiatives. Though the steel industry in India was experiencing slow growth, Tata Steel was able to post high profits because of its strong B2C and B2B sales.

Exhibit II: Tata Steel's Modernization Program

Phase–I (1981-85; Rs.2.3 billion)

- Installation of two 130t LD (Basic Oxygen Furnace) converters (a new technology of making steel in the place of open-hearth furnaces which had gone past their life cycle).
- Six strand continuous billet caster—a first in an integrated steel plant in India—to replace ingot making (continuous casting was a major technological breakthrough in the steel industry in the sixties).
- 130t vacuum arc refining un—again a first—to produce higher quality steel.

Phase–II (1985-92; Rs. 2.69 billion)

- Installation of 0.3 Mtpa wire rod mill to enrich the product mix.
- Blending plant for raw materials to improve the sinter quality.
- Sinter plant of 2.5 Mtpa capacity to increase sinter usage in blast furnaces.
- Coke oven battery with 54 ovens using stamp charging technology—again a first in India.
- Waste recycling plant of 1 Mtpa capacity for ecological considerations.
- Coal injection in blast furnaces—first in India—to reduce coke consumption.

Phase–III (1992-96; Rs.36 billion)

- Installation of two more stamp charged coke oven batteries.
- Installation of a new 1 Mtpa blast furnace—the best blast furnace in India.
- Installation of another LD shop (LD2) with two 130t combined blown converters to eliminate open hearths completely and to augment the production of continuously cast slabs from two single stand slab casters catering to the production of flat products.
- Installation of new hot strip mill (initially of 1 Mtpa capacity), to allow Tata Steel to enter the more profitable flat product market.

Phase–IV (1996-2000; Rs.12.62 billion)

- Increase in hot metal and crude steel capacity.
- Third-130t vessel at LD 2.
- Third-single stand slab caster to allow 100% continuous casting.
- Doubling of hot strip mill capacity to produce more flat steel.

Source: www.tatasteel.com

KM Initiatives at Tata Steel

The KM program at Tata Steel was started in 1999. The aim of the program was to tap the abundant knowledge base in the form of tacit knowledge[15] and explicit knowledge[16] that was lying unused, and make it available for use across the company. The KM process was started by bringing together a group of people with exposure in different fields, but completely inexperienced in implementing KM. The company felt that KM was a cultural transformation rather than a project. Thus involving a group of people from within the company with the support of top management was likely to be more effective in implementing the KM strategy, than hiring people from outside.

The next step involved establishing a knowledge repository where all the employees would participate actively. This repository was placed on the corporate intranet[17] and all the employees shared their experiences of successes and failures in implementing projects. Employees were encouraged to participate actively in the knowledge management program through a Knowledge Piece (KP) or query on the KM site through the intranet. After verification by an expert, their contribution was posted on the site. If there was query by any employee, the author responded and the process was closed only after the person inquiring was satisfied with the answer (refer Figure I for KM System at Tata Steel). For

Exhibit III: Performance Ethic Program

The Performance Ethic Program (PEP) aims at redesigning structures and processes in the organization to encourage high performance from employees. It also focuses on motivating managers to bring out the best in them. The PEP initiative consists of two basic elements:

- Creating a new organizational structure, and
- Introduction of performance management systems.

According to company sources, the new organizational structure would aim to cultivate growth, a flexible decision-making process and accountability. It would also try to inculcate a team spirit among employees. The new performance management systems would focus on reward systems that would be linked to performance, and offer self-development opportunities to all employees equally.

Additionally, under this initiative, the Tata Steel management would define the job profiles of all employees, bringing transparency in performance appraisals so that the best performers would be given rewards.

Source: www.tatasteel.com

more effective KM, Tata Steel integrated the knowledge repositories at the division/department level with the main KM repository.

After the creation of knowledge repository, the next step was forming knowledge communities (refer Exhibit IV for the stages of KM at Tata Steel). Knowledge communities were formed one year after the knowledge repository was established. Knowledge communities gave a forum to like-minded people to meet and share their experiences. Knowledge communities were not problem-solving platforms, but groups of people who came together to share their knowledge and to learn from one another through their experiences. Sometimes, the knowledge communities took up a problem and solved it by brainstorming. Knowledge communities were not aimed at short-term gains, but were an investment for the company's future.

Revamped Strategy

Though Tata Steel did make a good beginning in KM, there were some problems which were not addressed (refer Exhibit V for factors required for successful KM implementation). Connectivity was still poor and access technology was not standardized. Many irrelevant contributions were being made to the knowledge repositories. Said Ravi Arora (Arora), head of KM at Tata Steel, Worse, there were

Figure II

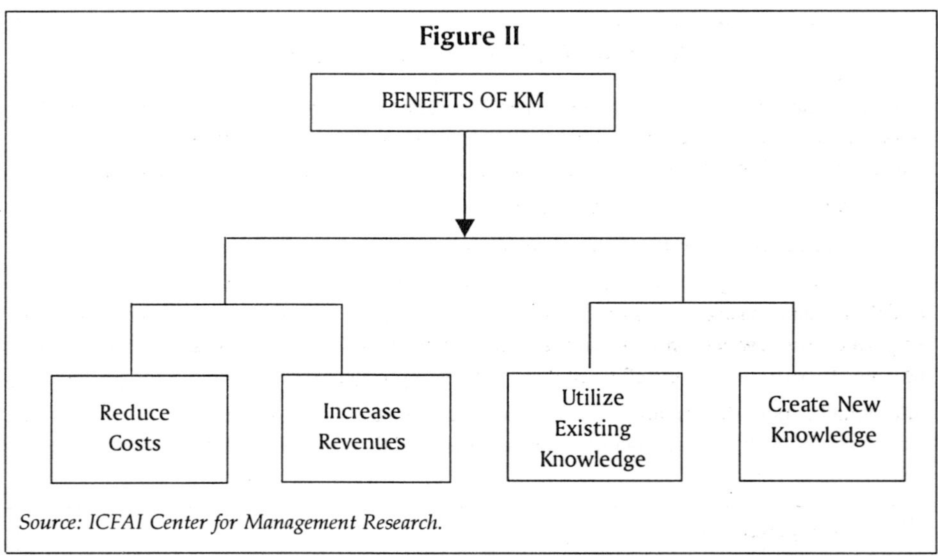

Source: ICFAI Center for Management Research.

cultural problems with technology phobias and attitudes such as, "This is another method to downsize" and "Why should I share my precious knowledge?"[18]

In May 2000, Tata Steel adopted a refined strategy for KM. It started organizing seminars on KM and identifying and recognizing some successful KM efforts made by employees in the organization. In the same year, the company hired McKinsey consultants for advice on communities of practice. Communities of practice were established to work towards capturing the tacit knowledge of experts, improving the quality of the knowledge repository and encouraging usage of the repository. These communities included members playing five important roles, viz., Champion,[19] Convener,[20] Practice Leader,[21] Lead Expert[22] and Practitioner.[23] The communities focused on 21 areas including iron making, steel making, rolling, maintenance, mining, waste management, cost engineering, and energy management. Employees were free to join any of the communities, irrespective of the area they belonged to.

In spite of all these changes, only 240 users in 2000-01 felt that the available knowledge was useful and could be applied in their area of work, and in

Exhibit IV: Phases of KM @ Tata Steel

Phase–1 (1999-2000)	**Phase–2 (2000-01)**	**Phase–3 (2001-02)**	**Phase–4 (2002 Onwards)**
Create awareness	Knowledge communities kickoff	Design KM index	Involvement of supervisors
Design processes	Security system in KM portal introduced	Design community index	Focus on knowledge creation by communities
Design systems		Deploy KM Processes across Organization	Virtual communities
Launch of KM portal		"Ask Expert" launched	Customer and supplier knowledge
Create success stories		Recognition system introduced	

Source: Adapted from www.tatasteel.com

Exhibit V: Factors Required for Successful KM Implementation

1. Connectivity

KM practice can be successful only through the best of use of technology. The technology provides the infrastructure for knowledge sharing, and this KM architecture should be available throughout the organization.

2. Content

The internal and external knowledge base of the organization must be assessed before launching a formal KM system. This way, an organization can assess the knowledge content available with the organization.

3. Community

Communities of practice or groups of people with similar interests contribute in a major way to the success of a KM system.

4. Culture

Support and vision from top management, a shared sense of direction, trust, openness, excitement, and a willingness to continually learn from peers are key components of KM culture.

5. Co-operation

Co-operation is a key success factor, especially in order to overcome cultural, linguistic and other barriers that arise in companies operating across the globe.

6. Capacity

In addition to having a willingness to share and learn, an organization must have the "intellectual capital governance" capacity to take KM to a higher stage. This governance capacity must be deployed to build the necessary skill sets and systematically execute a KM strategy. Sometimes, the in-house capacity for KM needs to be assessed by an outside KM consultancy.

7. Commerce

Commercial and other incentives to embrace change in a knowledge economy must be implemented, and systems of appraisal and rewards for outstanding contributions through the repository and user answers in a KM system need to be introduced.

8. Capital

All the above need a huge capital investment by the company. The capital to be deployed is decided on the basis of the returns expected computed using appropriate investment metrics.

Source: www.destinationkm.com

1999-2000, only 100 feedbacks were received. Company officials were of the opinion that these numbers were too small for a company of the size of Tata Steel. The need of the hour was to improve the quality of knowledge available and to inculcate among the employees the habit of browsing, so that they could acquire the knowledge stored and use it.

With this objective in mind, in January 2001, Tata Steel introduced an index called the "KM Index", to measure the performance of the system and reward successful KM initiatives taken by any employee. Each officer of the company was expected to score a minimum of 130 points on the KM Index. The scoring system would change, as the company evolved towards using knowledge proactively. In 2001-02, 70 points were assigned for making a valuable contribution to the Knowledge Repository, 30 points were assigned to one-time feedback, interaction or collaboration with the author of another KP, and another 30 points were assigned for the application of a KP from the site. In 2002-03, the scoring pattern was to be revised, and it was decided that by the time the organization became a true learning organization with free flow of knowledge and information sharing, the points system would be done away with.

In early 2002, Tata Steel introduced a stringent monitoring system for KM activity. Employees started browsing the knowledge management pages more frequently. On the cultural front, employee attitudes transformed from one of, "I am an expert, I do not need new knowledge" to one of a continuous quest for knowledge; from just, "I need help" to "I can also help."[24] According to Arora, "The extent of organizational knowledge changed from narrow and shallow silos to wider and more permeable silos."[25]

To increase the effectiveness of KM, Tata Steel made two major changes in the organization. As a first step, performance evaluation of employees was linked to KM. The senior executives of the company started using a balanced scorecard[26] to monitor the performance of employees, divisions in the KM process, and for taking corrective measures to improve the implementation of KM. As a second step, Tata Steel also launched a formal rewards and recognition system for KM. The CEO rewarded the best performing employee, team and knowledge community.

Benefits Reaped from KM

Generally, any KM implementation has two sets of benefits (refer Figure II). First, it reduces the cost of production and consequently increases the revenue, and second, it leads to utilization of existing knowledge and creation of new knowledge.

In addition to these, Tata Steel reaped other benefits too. Collaboration, conversation and interaction among employees increased, experts' skills were available throughout the organization; job satisfaction among the employees increased and this reduced the loss of intellectual capital; expenditure on R&D was reduced as new ideas were generated from within the organization; duplication of ideas being used across the organization was reduced; productivity increased as knowledge was available more quickly and easily and innovations were encouraged. Above all, KM allowed Tata Steel to gain a competitive advantage in the marketplace.

Future of KM at Tata Steel

In the future, Tata Steel plans to link e-learning with the KM repository and KM communities, devise an intellectual capital index, network with retired employees, and develop employee skills for better externalization of knowledge and integration with the customer's knowledge. According to company sources, "The most important challenge in this economy is creating conversations." According to Arora, "The key to business modernization in the 21st century is not just through the expenditure of huge sums of money to create physical assets, but orienting people—the greatest asset—towards meeting the opportunities and challenges of the future." Tata Steel seemed to be well placed to achieve its mission which was redrafted in 1998 to include the statement: "Tata Steel enters the new millennium with the confidence of a learning and knowledge-based organization."[27]

Endnotes

1 www.tatasteel.com

2 www.tatasteel.com

3 Every year, two British organizations, Teleos and the KNOW Network, choose companies for their 'Most Admired Knowledge Enterprise' (MAKE) awards. Teleos is an independent company which conducts research on knowledge management, while the KNOW network is a virtual global community of organizations dedicated to networking, benchmarking and sharing of best knowledge practices.

4 Will be discussed later in the case.

5 Jamshedji Nusserwanji Tata (J N Tata) was the founder of the Tata Group of Companies.

6 Steel with less than 0.15% carbon is known as Mild Steel. It is also known as low-carbon steel and soft cast steel.

7 Initially Bokaro was in Bihar. Since 2000, Bokaro has been in Jharkhand, the new state carved out of Bihar.

8 Hot rolled coil is a coil of steel rolled on a hot-strip mill (hot-rolled steel). It can be sold in this form to customers or be processed further into other finished products. Cold rolling is a process where the shape and structure of the steel can be changed by rolling, hammering, or stretching it at a low temperature (often room temperature).

9 Interview with J. J. Irani, *Advertising & Marketing,* September 15, 2001.

10 Integrated steel producers have the facilities to manufacture steel, from the iron ore stage right up to the finished steel stage.

11 ISO 14000 is a series of environmental management standards developed and published by the International Organization for Standardization (ISO) for organizations. The ISO 14000 standards provide guidelines or framework for organizations that need to systematize and improve their environmental management efforts. The ISO 14000 standards are not designed to aid the enforcement of environmental laws and do not regulate the environmental activities of organizations. Adherence to these standards is voluntary.

12 In September 2003, Rs.45.91 equaled 1 US dollar.

13 An industry analysis firm based in the US.

14 The EVA of a company is positive when the return on net assets (RONA) is greater than the cost of the capital invested.

15 Invisible knowledge that is confined to the mind of a person. It is hard to formalize and, therefore, difficult to communicate to others.

16 Knowledge which takes a visible form such as letters, reports, memos, literatures, etc. Explicit knowledge can be embedded in objects, rules, systems, methods, etc.

17 A network through which all the departments of Tata Steel at different locations were connected.

18 Madanmohan Rao, *Tempering Knowledge,* destinationKM.com

19 Someone who actively drives the knowledge agenda forward and creates enthusiasm and commitment.

20 Someone who develops a framework of knowledge management.

21 Person who encourages people to make active use of the knowledge base and expert skills available.

22 This person contributes actively to the knowledge repository and makes his expert skills available throughout the organization.

23 Person who makes the best use of knowledge management for solving his/her problems, through the use of the knowledge available in the repository.

24 Madanmohan Rao, *Tempering Knowledge,* www.destinationKM.com

25 Madanmohan Rao, *Tempering Knowledge,* www.destinationKM.com

26 The balanced scorecard is a management system (not only a measurement system) that enables organizations to clarify their vision and strategy and translate them into action. It provides feedback around both the internal business processes and external outcomes in order to continuously improve strategic performance and results.

27 www.tatasteel.com

Additional Readings & References

1. Jerry Ash, "State of the art among early adopters of Knowledge Management", Knowledge Inc., August 1997, www.kwork.org.
2. D.Raitt, S.Loekken, J.Scholz, H.Steinner and P.Sechhi, "Corporate Knowledge Management and Related initiatives at ESA", November 1997.
3. Karl-Erik Sveiby, "Knowledge Management: Lessons from the Pioneers", November 2001, www.sveiby.com
4. Seminar on Knowledge Management at Tata Steel, 1 February 2002, www.prodomain.com
5. "Siemens Selects Open Text's Livelink for Global Collaborative Knowledge Management," *Business Wire,* February 6, 2002.
6. Benefits of Knowledge Management, April 1, 2002, www.brint.com
7. Partnership to Provide Customers Comprehensive Collaboration and KM Solutions, *Business Wire,* July 15, 2002.
8. Madanmohan Rao, "Eight Keys to Successful KM Practice", August 23, 2002, www.kmadvantage.com
9. Madanmohan Rao, *Tempering Knowledge,* December 2, 2002, www.destinationkm.com
10. Knowledge Management implementation guide, Siemens, 2002.
11. Tata Steel recognized for KM, 9 March 2003, www.knowledgebusiness.com
12. Kingsley Martin, "FindLaw's Modern Practice—Evaluating the Benefits of Knowledge Management", April 2003, practice.findlaw.com
13. Radhika Sachdeva, "Buying in Knowledge Management", August 7, 2003, www.hindustantimes.com.
14. Asia's most admired knowledge enterprise, www.wkforum.org, 14 October 2003.
15. Tata Steel wins Asian Most Admired Knowledge Enterprises Award, October 16, 2003, www.tata.com
16. The Importance of Knowledge Management, www.mpmagazine.com, November 4, 2003.
17. David Skyrme, *Succeeding with Knowledge Management Workshop,* www.skyrme.com
18. Knowledge Management: the Basics, www.skyrme.com
19. Developing a knowledge management strategy, David Skyrme, classweb.gmu.edu
20. Have a Zest for Ideas? Revel in Knowledge Management, www.tatasteel.com
21. Seminar on Knowledge Management at Tata Steel, www.tatasteel.com
22. Benefits from Knowledge Management initiatives, www.sssi.net

23. Knowledge Management Maturity Model, Siemens corporate department technology.
24. Alan Ellison, "Information Transfer at Shell", www.informationtransfer.com
25. Kate Andrews, "KM in focus", www.bdokendalls.com.au
26. Swen Mehta, "Harness the I-capital before it drains", www.Indiabschools.com.
27. www.brint.com
28. www.kmworld.com
29. www.destinationkm.com
30. www.tatasteel.com
31. www.kmresource.com
32. www.knowledgeboard.com
33. www.outsights.com

14

KM Initiatives in India: Key Success Drivers

Swati Raman

This paper provides a pragmatic view of knowledge management initiatives and their implementation in organizations. It highlights various tools, techniques and strategies adopted by organizations to operationalize their knowledge management initiatives. It delves into the real-life examples to carve out valuable insights regarding all that goes into the creation of an organizational culture that is directed towards continuous learning and innovation.

In an economy where the only certainty is uncertainty, the one sure source of competitive advantage is knowledge. When markets shift, technologies proliferate, competitors multiply, and products become obsolete almost overnight, successful companies are those that consistently create new knowledge, disseminate it widely throughout the organization, and quickly embody it in new technologies and products.

— Nonaka (1991)[1]

In an era where business scenario is characterized by intense volatility and severe upheavals, the organizations are facing threats to their survival. The business environment has become highly unpredictable thus leaving no room for relying on forecasts. In such an environment, organizations have to be highly flexible, sprightly, responsive and adaptive. The need to evolve with the changing marketplace has made it vital for organizations to focus on continuous learning and innovation. The static and rigid structures are replaced by flexible and dynamic learning organizations. The organizations are streamlining and integrating their internal processes to foster a culture of continuous learning. These factors have led to the burgeoning of a new era of knowledge economy.

Once considered a fad, 'knowledge management' has evolved to take on a critical role in the business arena. Now more and more organizations have realized the vitality of the concept of 'knowledge management'. They are rejuvenating their organization by stimulating a spirit of learning and innovation. The organizations are now evolving various systems and procedures for managing their intellectual resources effectively. An enquiry into the success of knowledge management initiatives in the various firms across the world leads to a conclusion that sustainable competitive advantage comes from what the organization collectively knows and how efficiently it uses what it knows, besides readily acquiring and using new knowledge.

Objective

Knowledge has emerged as the key differentiating factor and a source of sustainable competitive advantage for organizations. This paper is an effort to take a pragmatic look on the knowledge management issues and challenges facing organizations worldwide. It draws upon the practical experiences of some world-class organizations to explore the essentials of a knowledge management initiative. The focus of enquiry for this paper is centered on the essentials of a KM system, critical issues in KM implementation and critical success factors for an effective and efficient KM initiative. Drawing upon the learning from some globally successful organizations, this paper highlights the essential components of knowledge management programs in organizations.

Methodology

The methodology of this paper involves scrutinizing the available literature on the related issues and company analysts' reports. Extensive literature survey adopting a case-based approach was done to cull out intended information. It draws upon the secondary information to study two organizations and their KM initiatives in great depth. It is an exploratory study, which purely tries to dig and probe into real-life experiences of various organizations to generate some important implications for empirical studies.

Conceptual Background

Firms need to capitalize on their knowledge base to derive a sustainable competitive advantage. Over the years, the practitioners have given a number of explanations and offered several definitions to explain what exactly they mean by knowledge management (KM). They have reached a consensus that KM is a true practice involving people, process and technology. As Davenport puts it, KM refers to "processes of capturing, distributing and effectively using its knowledge."[2] The term 'management' in KM refers to entire gamut of processes involving planning, organizing, handling, directing, controlling and coordinating of all the knowledge resources available in the organization. Capturing and integrating knowledge within systems is more challenging than creating knowledge.

Rebecca O Barkely and Philip C Murray at *Knowledge Praxis,* define knowledge management as "a business activity with two primary aspects:

- Treating the knowledge component of business activities as an explicit concern of business reflected in strategy, policy, and practice at all levels of the organization.
- Making a direct connection between an organization's intellectual assets —both explicit [recorded] and tacit [personal know-how]—and positive business results."[3]

Thus KM is all about leveraging the existing knowledge to create value for the organizations. IT helps in fostering innovation by encouraging the free flow of ideas and thoughts. An effective KM results in improved efficiency, higher productivity and increased revenues in all functions and operations being carried out in the firm.

Knowledge Management Systems (KMS) refer to a set of interactions among the various subsystems for identifying, capturing, producing and maintaining organization's knowledge base. The system aims at bringing people together on an interactive forum, to facilitate free flow of information and knowledge, which add value to the business. The KMS also helps in mapping and benchmarking expertise to create communities of practice. The systems enable people to share their work-related experiences and best practices, which might enhance the operational efficiency of other people. Thus the hidden knowledge, which is expressed in terms of actions and behaviors of human beings, can be codified and shared throughout the system.

An organization aiming to launch a KM initiative usually involves the processes of coding and sharing of practical/on-job experiences and best practices. The exact process of KM has still not been codified, as there has been a lot of debate on this concept. But just to offer a simplistic explanation, it can be said that an ideal KMS involves five stages:

- The first stage involves discovering organizational knowledge through personal intervention, socialization, etc.
- Once discovered, the knowledge needs to be embodied and realized within the organization.
- The captured knowledge is then stored in systems from where they can be retrieved as and when need arises.
- Some knowledge might become redundant for the organization within a due span of time. Thus the organization needs to ensure proper and timely disposal of such knowledge.
- And the most important step is creating a network for developing a common platform for interactions among the other components.

These steps help in evolving an efficient KMS. But to make the system function effectively, proper implementation of the program is also vital. To ensure proper diffusion, exploitation and capitalization of the knowledge base, an organization needs to concentrate on various perspectives, including the conceptual, procedural, organizational, technological and cultural perspectives. The feasibility of implementing and managing such a program should be carefully adjudged to develop an excellent knowledge management system within the organization and to reap maximum benefits from it.

KM Initiatives–Cases

The following section delves into the details of how an organization goes about creating and maintaining an effective and efficient KM system. It discusses the various initiatives taken up by these organizations to identify, capture and integrate available knowledge in their systems. It seeks to explain the various important factors and components, in terms of technologies, techniques and strategies that ensure proper functioning of the KM system. This section leads to valuable insights into all that goes into the creation of an organizational culture that is directed towards continuous learning and innovation.

KM at Wipro

Wipro, the technology services division of Wipro Ltd., entered the information technology field in 1980s. The organization specializes in enterprise IT development, and engineering work involving the design of software products that their clients will use internally or market to customers. Wipro, a knowledge-intensive organization, in its quest for creating business value and gain competitive advantage, felt the need of managing its organizational assets. The most important asset for Wipro was its vast knowledge base. Wipro was a multinational corporation having presence in different parts of the world involving wide varieties of culture and communities. Thus with the objective of tapping its intellectual assets and use the inherent strengths in people and processes, the company evolved a KM framework, which was applicable across culture, content, communities and business processes.

At Wipro, KM was believed to be a process of identifying the right set of business needs and leveraging existing investments in people and systems to deliver the right value to the organization. The process started at Wipro in early '90s focusing on small business units rather than the entire organization. The early knowledge-capturing and sharing mechanisms used by the organization were project systems (WILL and WISE). They were followed by quality initiatives under Veloci-Q. In 2001, they moved forward by adopting the i-Desk system. Mr. Maniram, Head of KM at Wipro, who took the initiative of enhancing the knowledge network said, "One of the challenges that I faced after taking over as the Head of KM initiative was the task of evangelizing KM internally." People were not sure as to what benefits would KM bring to them. Therefore, the organization felt the need of developing a KM culture where knowledge sharing was to be appreciated as being in everyone's best interest. It was a challenging task as it involved a paradigm shift in the organizational culture. Thus organization-wide Knowledge Management Programs were initiated in 2001.

Vision

Wipro started its KM journey with a vision of becoming an organization where knowledge-capture and sharing were the way to work, offering customers innovative products and services fast. It aimed at providing to its employees an environment of continuous learning and productivity improvements.

Strategy

The first step in this direction was building top management commitment and appointing a full-time, dedicated knowledge manager to head the KM team. The team started out with identifying the key business drivers, which needed to be addressed for ensuring success.

The key drivers,[4] which they identified, were:

- Competitive responsiveness: Wipro's ability to access existing information in time.
- Collaborative work culture: Working as a collaborative team, sharing best practices and avoiding reinvention and repeating mistakes.
- Shorter time-to-market: Shortened product and project life cycles.
- Capturing tacit knowledge: Minimizing loss due to attrition and mobility.

Focusing on these drivers, Wipro identified following objectives[5] for their KM initiative:

- People are the primary assets and it is necessary to capture and leverage people know-how and know-what.

- Increase the transfer of individual knowledge to the organization.
- Link people who have requisite tacit and explicit knowledge with those who need it.
- Leverage organizational knowledge: bring the right information to the right people in a context that addresses their challenges.
- Increase collaboration opportunities: enrich the exchange of tacit and explicit knowledge between people.
- Share best-known practices across the enterprise to be able to learn from failed efforts and provide a platform for knowledge re-use and innovation.
- The upfront investments should be limited and existing infrastructure put to use.

With these objectives in place, Wipro set out to become a complete learning organization. Wipro initiated its journey with a comprehensive knowledge audit, tool evaluation in June 2001. After this, various initiatives were implemented across the organization. It involved all components of people, process and technology.

The Initiative

The Head of KM constituted a team of 15 members, who represented different domains across the organization. These members were responsible for driving KM programs in their respective domains leading towards institutionalization of KM within the organization. Knowledge mentors were appointed along with this team who were entrusted with the responsibility of knowledge capturing. They ensured creation and capturing of explicit knowledge objects like white papers, proposals, reusable components and technical documents across the organization. Several other teams comprising line managers and practitioners were also identified across domains for reviewing the usability and comprehensiveness of all explicit knowledge objects.

Infrastructure

The organization equipped itself with the state-of-the-art solutions to enable anytime and anywhere learning. Wipro inculcated a strong process culture. The intranet portal of the organization provided a strategic platform for information, transactions and collaboration. It addressed the needs of varied audiences such as marketing and sales, project teams and technical teams. Notification engines ensuring workflow were also used. For capturing and sharing best practices across the entire organization, it started with the activities like VelociQ, Project Learning (iPAT) and e-Learning. The HR processes were also streamlined and automated using Wipro's own framework for employees and community and collaboration, I-Desk, etc. The e-Llearning program helped in the process of storing knowledge and delivering it across the entire organization. Extranets called 'Cocoon' and Sales Logix CRM system were used for capturing and sharing customer knowledge.

Connecting People to Content

Various tools and techniques were instituted to make appropriate content available to people anytime anywhere. KNET was one such tool which provided a platform for enabling collaboration between various teams across Wipro. The KNET hosted numerous documents like case studies, presentations, whitepapers, etc., from various domains. The company launched a sales support KM system in November 2001 to make key information readily available to sales and support staff. It helped them respond to customer queries quickly and thus remove any existing inefficiencies. This needed support for multiple document types and involved integration with Wipro's existing CRM and sales systems. It provided for quicker search time for information required to respond to customer queries, ready access to information across all domains, latest and updated statistics about Wipro like latest market capitalization, number of employees, etc. Another support system known as TecNet was launched in April 2002, which acted as a forum of sharing information across all technical resources of Wipro. It was a repository of technical documents, evaluation reports and best practice documents. This system aimed at reducing rework and ensuring better and quicker completion of development and technical projects.

Reusable Components Repository was another such tool that aimed at eliminating redundant development of functionality and hence realizing business benefits. It allowed employees to share components that were developed to ensure quicker time to market on subsequent similar projects. Besides these, KM-based project system involved integration by providing instant access to all project information and to engage teams in a collaborative work environment.

Connecting People to People

The company also focused on creating a system to ensure externalization and socialization of knowledge residing in the minds of people. Creation of communities and special interest groups helped in exploiting tacit knowledge by getting people having similar interests to come together and share their knowledge and best practices. An efficient system named Yellow Pages/Find-the-Expert was instituted which involved profiling of all employees as regards their expertise and area of operation. This required integration of HRMS with SAP system. It helped building bridges between people who are in need of expertise and people who have expertise.

Measuring KM Effectiveness

The KM framework of Wipro ensured continuous feedback into the system. The knowledge cycle ensured that the learnings and knowledge gained are fed back into the system. This allowed the organization continuously refocus KM strategy, the key business processes and infrastructure. Six Sigma tools were used to gauge the effectiveness and engagement of all KM initiatives. The objective of this program was to continuously enhance the quality of user experience.

Reward & Recognition System

To institutionalize KM programs across organization and ensure active participation of all employees, Wipro devised a comprehensive reward and recognition system. It helped create an environment for sharing of knowledge and ideas and motivate employees through rewards and recognition for their efforts towards knowledge sharing.

Wipro was relatively new to the IT business at the time it initiated its KM Program. But through years, by constant monitoring and focus on quality assurance it evolved as one of the best KM systems across the world. Wipro has been able to benchmark its performance against top international standards. In 2002, Wipro won the KM reality award instituted by KM World for being the best practitioner of KM systems.

KM at Infosys

Founded in 1981, Infosys emerged as a Titan of the global software industry by carefully designing and constructing a unique corporate culture. The emerging information technology (IT) center at Bangalore, Infosys became the first Indian company to be listed on the NASDAQ in 1999. It is a leading provider of consulting and IT services with a wide range of services for technology driven business transformation initiatives.

Infosys began its knowledge management initiative with a mission to ensure that all organizational learning is leveraged in delivering business advantage to the customer.[6] For leveraging the organization-wide learning it was imperative to consolidate the knowledge and make it available to everybody in the organization. Following the 'learn once, use anywhere' motto, Infosys instituted an integrated approach to the management of knowledge. It was aimed at minimizing effort in redoing learning that has already happened elsewhere.

KM Vision

The objective behind Infosys' KM program was that every instance of learning within the system should be made available to every Infoscion. The program intended to provide every Infoscion the full backing of organization's learning in customer fronting, planning and decision-making and internal customer service. The KM vision is "to be an organization where every action is fully enabled by the power of knowledge; which truly believes in leveraging knowledge for innovation; where every employee is empowered by the knowledge of every other employee; and which is globally respected knowledge leader."[7]

Key KM Drivers

The KM initiative of Infosys is aimed at the objective that, 'as the company climbs the value curve, it increasingly needs effective mechanisms for speedy and efficient consolidation of expertise.'[8] The key drivers of the KM initiative at Infosys are as follows:

- To ensure better quality.
- Better revenue productivity through reuse, cycle time reduction, virtual teamwork, etc.

- Reducing risk by diversifying into new technologies, domains, geographical areas, services and resource interchangeability.
- To create greater market awareness.
- To ensure higher revenue growth.
- To increase customer satisfaction.

Knowledge Deployment Architecture

The KM architecture revolved around three key constituents—content, people and technology. Institutionalizing the KM initiatives was a complex activity. Thus the organization adopted a staged model of implementation modeled after the famous SEI-CMM model. It was named KMM (Knowledge Management Maturity) Model, which was based on the realization that the path to achieving KM success involves significant change in culture, process and systems. (Refer Annexure–I) KMM has five levels, which are characterized by certain Key Result Areas (KRAs) around people, content and technology. The purpose of KM model[9] was twofold:

1. To provide a framework which can be used to assess current level of KM maturity.
2. To act as a mechanism to focus and help prioritize efforts to raise the level of KM maturity.

The KMM helped the organization address the challenges of institutionalizing KM. The KM architecture, as mentioned earlier, had three constituents, which are described below:

The content architecture comprising K assets was classified into two groups according to their types. The first type of content is internal content, which represents Infosys' internal expertise, like BoK, White papers, reports, reusable codes and other artifacts, discussion groups, chat sessions, etc. The other is the external content, which represents expertise outside Infosys, including reviewed websites, glossaries of business and technology terms, technology summaries, on-line journals and books, external white papers and reports, etc. The flow of content into the repositories were charted, and envisaged different stages such as review by identified internal experts, streamlining and editing, publishing, certification and maintenance.

The technology architecture was characterized by the relationship between the central KM repositories and satellite repositories in various practice units, the organization's intranet, extranet, etc. A central KM portal was developed to provide ready access to the K assets. The portal thus planned to include:

- Integration of K-sharing applications like BoK, process assets, etc.
- A window to the Internet to facilitate the information gathering from the Internet, with reviewed websites and Internet search help.
- To allow navigation and search through websites maintained by various competency groups, business units, projects, etc.
- Including extra features like discussion groups and chat rooms, user reviews, ratings for content, news snippets, etc.

The people architecture was created to strike a balance between the functions managed by central KM group, and those that were performed in a decentralized manner. A central KM group was formed, which managed the technology architecture for the KM development, deployment and maintenance. It managed all stages of content development and usage.

The Initiative

Infosys started the organization wide KM program in a comprehensive manner. Initially, the organization faced four major challenges:[10]

- Promoting a sharing culture.
- Building and sustaining momentum.
- Deploying IT infrastructure.
- Ensuring quality and currency of content.

A number of initiatives were undertaken to address these issues and to institutionalize the practice of KM. A reward and recognition system called the Knowledge Currency Units (KCU) was designed. This scheme was meant to incentivize knowledge-sharing and rating the quality of assets in the repository. It acted as a virtual currency earned by participation in the KM program.

Whenever a member contributed a K asset, an authorized reviewer reviewed it and awarded appropriate KCUs to the assets and its author after judging its suitability. Any reader who read the asset and gained something from it could also award KCUs to the asset and the author. These KCUs later got translated into taxable perks for the contributor. When the asset earned a minimum amount of KCUs, it was certified as premium asset and was shared on the extranet.

The company instituted Sir Issac Newton Award for the projects going on within the organization. It was an annual award meant for projects, which made significant value addition in terms of clearly identifiable business advantages like cycle time reduction, lowering cost to customers, reducing response time to RFI and RFP, enhancing customer satisfaction. Besides this, all Infoscions were required to fill in weekly activity report (WAR) to record the proportion of time spent on each activity as well as time spent on KM activities. This data was later integrated with the performance appraisal system. A forum was constituted where any Infoscion could register himself as expert (operational) or guru (planned). A People Knowledge Map was also designed, which acted as Yellow Pages and helped in locating people and their expertise. Branding and promotion efforts were undertaken for marketing the KM program internally. The branding efforts included promoting the usage of K shop, conducting periodic summits, seminars, best practice sessions, on-line expert moderated chats, etc. Mementos like coffee mugs, t-shirts, etc., with a KM logo on it were distributed for promoting the KM program.

The IT Infrastructure

A robust and secure technology infrastructure was created by the central KM group, technology manager and the internal IS group for facilitating knowledge-sharing and use. The KM Portal called K Shop was managed by the KM group. It ensured organization wide dissemination of distributed learning across projects/practice units, while still retaining the ownership with the individual contributors, projects and practice units.

Body of Knowledge

This initiative was started in 1993 for establishing a formal system of sharing technical and experiential knowledge. The Infoscions were asked to document their experiences in the form of MS Word documents, which were to be collected and shared across the entire organization. Thus Body of Knowledge (BoK) essentially acted as a repository of experiential knowledge gained through various projects. The contributions to the BoK were reviewed for content and applicability aspects. Meritorious contributions were also awarded. Besides this project and practice unit, specific BoKs were also instituted.

Process Assets

Process assets constituted specific reusable assets generated for a particular project but stored for use by other projects as well. These were reusable artifacts with well-documented specific information that could be used in other projects. These assets are then captured in an intranet-based repository to minimize duplication of efforts in the creation of such assets in other projects. As a part of project closure, the project leaders were required to fill in a brief description of the project, the target audience and other project details while uploading into the system. This helped in classification and focused research. All assets were archived on the basis of the type of processes used in the project, viz., re-engineering process, development process, maintenance process, etc. This categorization aided in easy search and retrieval of relevant assets.

People Knowledge Maps

It was the intranet-based knowledge directory, which help in locating expertise within the organization. The company-wide intranet called 'Sparsh' acted as a central information portal. It consisted of about 5000 nodes, spread throughout the various India-based development centers and the US-based marketing offices. Sparsh had a knowledge shop that provided access to intranet-based knowledge systems. It also acted as a link between projects, PU, department and personal web pages.

Infosys gained remarkable success in KM implementation and won the Most Admired Knowledge Enterprises award in the Asian region for 2002 for its mature knowledge management practices.

Analysis and Findings

Quantifying the returns from a KM initiative is a difficult task and lacks accuracy. Therefore, the organizations have to rely on certain critical factors, the knowledge of which is generally derived from the experiences of others who are already practicing the art. But what works for one might not work for all. These experiences just work as a general guideline for those who want to frame their own systems. And for evolving one's own systems, the organizations have to modify the systems according to their own needs and requirements.

As seen in the above two cases, the process of implementing a KM system starts from identifying the knowledge requirements of the business and comparing it with the existing knowledge base to identify the knowledge gap. The organizations also need to study the external environment and the competing firms to determine their knowledge needs for gaining a sustainable competitive advantage. Having known the internal and external gaps, KM system needs to be evolved. The system should focus around the vision that should be operationalized in terms of clearly specified and measurable goals. It should not only act as a guideline but also help in measuring and evaluating the effectiveness of a KM initiative.

A typical implementation of KM begins with deciding upon the knowledge architecture. Thereafter, the decisions regarding systems and technology are to be made and finally deal with the people issues. Strict adherence to time schedule is necessary for aligning the architecture and systems and technology. And people-related issues are to be handled simultaneously. A successful KM system is generally characterized by the following attributes:

- Growth in assets and resources including staffing and budgets.
- Growth in K assets, contents and usage, which ensures participation of all employees.
- Acceptance and comfort in the organization with the concepts and practices of KM.
- Enhancement in returns in terms of reduction in cycle time, reduction in wastage and growth in profits of the organization.

A study of the various KM initiatives of the two most successful organizations practicing KM revealed some critical success factors, which are crucial for success of any such initiative. Though the success depends on numerous factors, the following are the most common issues found across all the organizations:

Clarity of Vision

Clarity of vision and purpose is one of the most vital success factors. People should be made aware of what knowledge management is and what is expected of them in the garb of KM and organizational learning. People are required to know how a KM system is going to benefit them and how they can add value to the organization by actively contributing to the system.

Top Management Commitment

Knowledge management involves a cultural transformation for which a strong support of executives is extremely vital. Support in terms of defining the focus of KM program, building awareness and commitment among employees, funding the infrastructure and clarifying goals and objectives etc., is required.

Cultural Orientation

A strong and robust knowledge-oriented culture is basic requirement for any KM initiative. Building knowledge-friendly culture is a challenging task. The most important factors of establishing a positive K culture are the people that an organization attracts and hires.

People should be particularly interested in seeking and applying knowledge. The willingness to share knowledge is critical to success of the program. In order to get creative people to share their knowledge with their peers, organizations need to establish an effective rewards and recognition system. There needs to be a fit between the culture and the initiative.

Infrastructural Support

The success of knowledge project depends on the availability of proper technological and organizational infrastructure. Appropriate systems and technologies need to be made available, depending on the form of knowledge object and the type and location of users. A strong IT infrastructure needs to be augmented. Effective knowledge-oriented tools and technologies need to be provided, besides a uniform set of technologies for desktop computing and communications. It means provision of a capable, networked PC on every desk with standardized productivity tools to ensure easy exchange of knowledge throughout the organization. The organizational infrastructure means establishing a set of roles, organizational structures, and skills from which the individual projects can benefit. Some firms established a multiple levels of new roles, like chief knowledge officer, knowledge managers, facilitators, editors, etc.

Linkage with Economic Benefit

Institutionalizing KM system in an organization is an expensive affair. Therefore, it needs to be linked to economic benefit and industry success. The returns from the initiatives may or may not be quantifiable. The benefits may involve the earnings or savings. Indirect benefits like customer satisfaction, reduction in cycle time, and reduction in number of complaints are also the indication of success in KM.

Motivational Aids

Employees need to be motivated to create, share and use knowledge. A well-planned and efficient incentives and rewards system needs to be established. It is necessary to create a willingness among people to share knowledge, because the common understanding among people is that knowledge is their personal asset. And they might lose their value to the organization by sharing it. Thus it is important to help them get over this feeling and be open to sharing it with their peers.

Structured Knowledge

All knowledge available in the organization should be properly structured. The assets in the repositories need to be classified and categorized on the basis of content and usability to ensure easy access to all those who need it. Devising a thesaurus and providing key terms may also assist users and make their search easier.

Multiple Channels for Knowledge Transfer

Knowledge can be transferred through various channels, either formal or informal. Thus for an organization to be successful, it is important to continuously reinforce each of them. For informal or face-to-face sharing, meetings or group activities need to be organized to facilitate open communication among people. Formal structures in the form of knowledge repositories, groupware and intranet, etc., are required for effective sharing across departmental, geographical and cultural boundaries.

Conclusion

In a rapidly changing business environment, it becomes imperative for the organizations to continuously learn and innovate. For surviving and thriving in the competitive scenario, organizations today are resorting to KM as their tool. An enquiry into the success of knowledge management initiatives in the various firms across the world leads to a conclusion that sustainable competitive advantage comes from what the organization collectively knows and how efficiently it uses what it knows, besides readily acquiring and using new knowledge. A successful KM practice needs an efficient collaboration and coordination between people, process and technology.

Organizations across the world are adopting various tools and techniques, to manage knowledge, which is their most critical asset. And since most part of this knowledge resides in the human brains, people form the most important component of the system. The top management needs to define a clear vision, develop a knowledge-intensive culture, and motivate people to create, share and use knowledge. A proper knowledge architecture and well-defined structure is required to build a platform for knowledge-creation and sharing. Technology intervention forms an important part of KM implementation. Various information technology tools like groupware, intranet, K repositories, K maps, etc, are used to facilitate the process. Efficient rewards and recognition systems need to be established to continuously motivate people to contribute to the system. The strategies adopted by most of the organizations are similar in nature. But not all of them are applicable to every organization. What works for one might not be useful for the other organizations. Each organization needs to evolve its own structure on the basis of its needs. Thus, it can be said that though the approach to KM remains the same but the tools keep changing from organization to organization.

In the end, the location of the new economy is not in the technology, be it the microchip or the global telecommunications network. It is in the human mind.

– By Alan Webber[11]

(Swati Raman, doctoral student, ICFAI Institute for Management Teachers, Hyderabad.)

Endnotes

1 Archana Shukla & R Srinivasan, "Designing Knowledge Management Architecture", 2002.

2 Joseph M Firestone, "Basic Concepts of Knowledge Management", White Paper No. 9, Executive Information Systems Inc., June 24, 1998.

3 Barkley, Rebecca O and Murray, Phillip C., "What is Knowledge Management?" *Knowledge Praxis,* Knowledge Management Association, 1997.

4 Rajakannu Manimaran, "Wipro's Collaboration and KM journey", White paper, Wipro Technologies.

5 ibid.

6 Archana Shukla & R Srinivasan, "Designing Knowledge Management Architecture", 2002.

7 ibid.

8 M Tenmozhi, "Knowledge Management in Knowledge Based Enterprises", *Knowledge Management: A New Dawn,* ICFAI Books, 2002

9 ibid.

10 Archana Shukla & R Srinivasan, "Designing Knowledge Management Architecture', 2002.

11 Davenport and Prusak, "Working Knowledge: How Organizations Manage What They Know", 1998.

References

Alavi Maryam, Leidner E. Dorothy, 'Review: Knowledge Management and Knowledge Management Systems: Conceptual Foundations and Research Issues', *MIS Quarterly,* Volume 25, No.1, March 2001.

Barnes Stuart, *Knowledge Management Systems: Theory & Practice,* 2002.

Cope Mick, 'Developing a Working Definition: Making the Cross over from Theory to Application', *KM Review,* March-April, 1998.

Davenport and Prusak, *'Working Knowledge: How Organizations Manage What They Know',* 1998.

Dr. Benjamin V Richards, 'Knowledge management in knowledge intensive organization',

White Paper, ISOCO, December 2001.

Garud Raghu, Kumaraswamy Arun, & Malhotra Monica, 'A passage from India', *Stern Business,* Spring Summer 2003.

Holowetzki Antonina, 'The Relationship Between Knowledge Management and Organizational Culture: An Examination of Cultural Factors that support the Flow & Management of Knowledge within an organization', AIM program, University of Oregon, December 2002.

Joseph M Firestone, 'Basic concepts of Knowledge Management', White Paper No. 9, Executive Information Systems Inc. June 24, 1998.

Malhotra Y, 'Knowledge Management and New Organizational Forms: A Framework for Business Model Innovation', *Information Resources Management Journal,* Volume 13, No. 1, January-March, 2000.

Maria Molina, Pak Yoongy, 'Knowledge Sharing in a Co-opetitive Environment: The Case of Business Clusters', *Journal of Information & Knowledge Management,* Vol. 2, No. 4 (2003).

M Tenmozhi, 'Knowledge Management in Knowledge Based Enterprises', *Knowledge Management: A New Dawn,* ICFAI Books, 2002

Pommier Michel J L, 'How the World Bank Launched a Knowledge Management Program', www.kwork.org

Rajakannu Manimaran, 'Wipro's Collaboration and KM journey', White paper, Wipro Technologies.

Shukla Archana & Srinivasan R, 'Designing Knowledge Management Architecture', 2002.

www.wipro.com

www.ciol.com

www.kmworld.com

www.kmresource.com

www.brint.com

www.infosys.com

Annexure–I: KRAs for Each Level of KMM Model

Level	Key Result Areas		
	People	**Content**	**Technology**
LEVEL 1 Default	–	–	–
LEVEL 2 Reactive	Knowledge awareness	Content capture	Basic information management
LEVEL 3 Aware	Central knowledge organization Knowledge education	Content structure management	Knowledge technology infrastructure
LEVEL 4 Convinced	Customized enabling	Content enlivement Knowledge configuration management Quantitative KM	Knowledge infrastructure management
LEVEL 5 Sharing		Expertise integration Knowledge leverage Innovation management	

15

From Community of Practice to On Demand Workplace: IBM's Journey in Knowledge Management

Jayaprada, Minita Sinha and T R Venkatesh

IBM set about its journey in KM in 1994 with the design of the ICM (Intellectual Capital Management) AssetWeb framework, which abided community of practice. After the success of community of practice in IBM, it was proposed as a knowledge management solution in the market. IBM Global Service realized the potency of knowledge management in their organization and was involved in research to develop an advanced knowledge management system. In 2003, On Demand Workplace was set up in IBM where employees could share and transfer knowledge across the globe. After the success of in-house On Demand Workplace, it was extended as a business solution to its clients in 2004.

Behind the scenes we've been re-engineering IBM from top to bottom, with one goal: to foster a high-performance culture and turn IBM into the world's premier knowledge management company.

– Lou Gerstner, Chairman and CEO, IBM in 1997.[1]

In 2004, IBM was the world's largest information technology and services company with revenue of 96 billion dollars. IBM Global Services, the largest unit of IBM, had played a very active role in starting the knowledge management initiative (Annexure I) within the organization to capture the valuable experiences and insights of employees. IBM Global Services had implemented a knowledge management initiative called community of practice to enhance communication and collaboration among employees.

The success of community of practice in IBM Global Services prompted IBM to offer it as a solution to its clients. The acceptance of this solution in the market encouraged Lou Gerstner, the then CEO of IBM, to invest in further research in the area of knowledge management. Gerstner felt that IBM should become more proactive in knowledge management activities and develop knowledge management systems[2] and related products. With that objective in mind, IBM developed a knowledge management system known as Lotus Discovery System which was successfully implemented in IBM and was offered as a product in 2001. But due to problems like incompatibility and pricing, it was withdrawn from the market in 2004.

Over the years, the work environment had improved with more sophisticated tools. Further, IBM had felt the need for a more sophisticated knowledge management tool. Therefore, in 2003, IBM implemented the On Demand Workplace, which consisted of different types of tools, to enhance the interaction of employees. After the success of On Demand Workplace in-house, it was offered as a business solution to its clients in 2004. IBM executives wondered on how On Demand Workplace would fare in the market and whether it would be accepted by the customer.

Company Background

International Business Machines Corporation (IBM), also known as Big Blue, started its operations in 1888 in Armonk, New York, USA, as a producer of punch card tabulating machines. In 1953, it introduced its first computer, the 701. IBM dominated the mainframe and minicomputer market during the '60s and the '70s. In 1981, it launched a series of personal computers which later became the industry standard. By 2004, IBM was into several products and services in information technology. IBM manufactured, developed and sold computer hardware, software and services. It offered services and skills in e-business, package integration[3] and knowledge management. IBM was also involved in nanotechnology[4] and grid computing.[5] It provided services to various industries including automotive, chemicals and petroleum, distribution, finance, insurance, and healthcare industries. With over 330,000 employees, it had its operations in more than 170 countries.

IBM grouped its various businesses into five units: Global Services, Hardware, Software, Global Financing, and Enterprise Investment. In 2004, the total revenue was $96 billion (Annexure II). As of 2004, IBM employed about 191,000 technical professionals in which 300-400 were distinguished engineers and 50-60 were IBM Fellows.[6] IBM also employed some of the best minds in the field of technology and science. On IBM's payroll, there were five recipients of Nobel prizes,[7] four of Turing Awards,[8] five of National Medals of Technology,[9] and five of National Medals of Science.[10]

Different development centers of IBM located across the world were involved in the development of middleware and hardware. IBM had also set up manufacturing plants and research labs in Europe and Asia Pacific including India, China and Japan to carry out research activities (Annexures III and IV). IBM entered the area of business consulting in 2002 by its acquisition of PricewaterhouseCoopers, renowned organization for financial and business consulting.[11] By 2004, under the leadership of Samual Palmisano, IBM had significantly strengthened its consulting and service activities. In fact, it earned more from this segment than it did from hardware and software segments.

IBM Global Services

IBM Global Services' mandate was to integrate services, hardware, software and research to help companies realize the full potential of information technology.[12] It offered services in areas like application development, data storage, infrastructure management, networking and technical support. It also provided business consulting and outsourcing services. As of 2004, IBM Global Services had 140,000 professionals serving customers in 160 countries.

On Demand Business solutions offered advanced technologies and flexible solutions on rent basis, to organizations whose core business was not information technology development. It was defined as a "company whose business processes—integrated end-to-end across the company and with key partners, suppliers and customers—could respond with flexibility and speed to any customer demand, market opportunity or external threat". One of the solutions that was offered in 2004 was On Demand Workplace to support knowledge management initiatives in IBM.

Exhibit I: Knowledge Management Services

Knowledge Management Services	Purpose
Institute of Knowledge Management	Research to advance the discipline of knowledge management.
Knowledge Strategy	Plans for knowledge management, puts emphasis on people.
Community-Based Services	Developed physical and virtual communities for problem solving, knowledge exchange and knowledge creation.
Community Knowledge Portal	Improved the productivity of knowledge workers through integrated access to enterprise information.
Human Capital Management	Management of employees.
Intellectual Capital Management	Helped to identify and retain the best people and ideas.
Organizational Network Analysis	Offered ways to measure knowledge flow, remove inefficiencies and build decision and innovation networks.
Competitive Intelligence	Offered tool to understand the competitive market.
Knowledge Retention in Mergers and Acquisitions	Helped to turn the perceived value added to knowledge boosters.
Knowledge Disclosure: Storytelling	Helped to convert tacit knowledge into explicit knowledge through storytelling.
Knowledge Management Technical Services	Ensured maximum knowledge management capabilities.

Source: Compiled by ICBR.

Exhibit II: The Knowledge Management Technologies	
Technology	**What it targets**
Business Intelligence	Data and text mining, OLAP, and data warehousing.
Collaboration	Groupware, synchronous mapping, e-mail
Knowledge transfer	Computer-based training, distributed learning, live collaboration.
Knowledge discovery and mapping	Search, classification/navigation, document management.
Expertise	Expert network, visualization, affinity identification.
Source: Lotus "Knowledge Management Products." www.ibm.com, 2001.	

Development of Knowledge Management in IBM

To enter the knowledge management domain, IBM had bought Lotus in 1994. IBM Global Services, with the help of Lotus products, was involved in many knowledge management activities (Exhibit I). The knowledge management initiative had started with the use of collaboration technology like groupware and e-mail (Annexure V). These technologies were used to build a knowledge management framework called Intellectual Capital Management (ICM) AssetWeb, in 1994. Together, IBM and Lotus identified five technologies that were essential for building knowledge management products (Exhibit II).

The products offered by IBM could be integrated with each other depending on customer requirement. A product could either work on one technology or was used as a combination of technologies to provide different functionalities. For example, Lotus Dominio TM supported collaboration and knowledge discovery. In 2004, IBM had more than 15 products (Annexure VI). In 2004, the knowledge management products that were offered by IBM Global Services were WebSphere Information Integrator[13] for integration of data and content and WebSphere Portals.

In 2004, IBM introduced On Demand Workplace that offered a knowledge-sharing space within the confines of the organization. Knowledge-sharing had started in 1994 through the development of communication and collaboration framework called Intellectual Capital Management AssetWeb.

Intellectual Capital Management AssetWeb

Intellectual capital consisted of tacit knowledge like know-how, experiences, wisdom, ideas and explicit knowledge like objects, code, models, and technical architectures. The ICM AssetWeb provided the infrastructure for IBM's knowledge management solutions and initiatives. The ICM AssetWeb captured the intellectual capital of IBM. Several tools like version management, multidatabase searching, "yellow pages", and user preference configurators were built in ICM AssetWeb. IBM continued to upgrade ICM AssetWeb with respect to technology and content. In 1998, The ICM AssetWeb had won the gold medal of the Giga Excellence Award on Knowledge Management.[14]

The objective of ICM AssetWeb was to capture information about customers from internal (meaning teams handling customer) as well as external sources. In ICM AssetWeb framework, intellectual capital was evaluated and stored in a structured form. The workflow and business processes were defined[15] in this framework. The framework supported community of practice for collaboration and teamwork.

Communities of Practice

In IBM, communities of practice were defined as groups of individuals who met on a regular basis to discuss different areas of expertise and interests. Communities of practice basically dealt with people aspect of the organization. ICM AssetWeb provided communication and collaboration tools to be used by the people of communities of practice.

Communities of practice in IBM helped to capture the skills and expertise of its employees throughout the world and stored it in a data repository. The presence of communities in IBM helped to reduce the time and expense that was spent on training the new as well as the old employees. Each community within IBM varied in issue, technology, process, participation and community development. It underwent different stages of formation (Annexure VII). Communities at IBM were able to adapt to the changing business environment, while maintaining their unique identity. The communities were also able to support and establish alliances with other communities or knowledge networks in related competencies.

In 2000, there were over 60 unique communities of practice and about 76,000 professionals who accessed the ICM AssetWeb.[16] About 20,000 employees were participating in community of practice. The level of participation and sustainability seemed to indicate a significant degree of success. In 2000, IBM Global Services announced the community-based services. These services provided collaborative and communication tools to its clients. It also helped the clients to develop communities of practice. Community-based services helped to provide support to those communities that were important to the organization.

As the technology advanced, the collaborative and communication tool, an integral part of community of practice, was developed and updated. This resulted in the design and development of Lotus Discovery System. The objective behind this system was the same as community of practice but it made it easier to organize, update, store, and maintain information.

Lotus Discovery System

Lotus Development Corp's Knowledge Discovery System 1.0 code named "Raven" was released in December 2000, in Lotusphere, Europe. It consisted of a portal[17] product K-station and K-Discovery server. Lotus K-station was a browser based collaborative portal through which business knowledge was acquired, shared, and transferred by users. In K-station portal, users were able to create personalized, web-accessible team workspaces. This portal had online awareness and real-time chat capabilities which helped the users to see who was online, connect with them and get fast answers to their queries.

Lotus Knowledge Discovery Server was released in April 2001, after the release of K-Station portal. It provided expertise on profiling and location, content cataloging and retrieval, search and knowledge audits. It could go through structured as well as unstructured content in order to extract, organize, and store the data. This server could also track relevant end-user activity and identify individuals best suited to address that task.

The Discovery Server had three major components: spiders, K-map and text retrieval engine. The spiders were the workers of the system. They gathered documents from the selected sources and monitored any changes like deletions that were done on these sources. The K-map was used to keep track of repositories[18] of data, by refining the categories for better control of content. The K-map made it easier to find the appropriate people or staff according to the project requirement through affinities, and it helped managers to keep track of expertise within the organization. The text retrieval engine created index, by breaking word into strings having uniform number of characters, for quick and efficient search.

The K-station was scalable, i.e., once one K-station server was installed, multiple servers could be added to the K-station. Installation of K-Station server was difficult as it did not install in any system that had Microsoft IIS.[19] If the setup program detected the presence of IIS files, it would terminate the setup process and the installation would not be completed. The integration required considerable administrative skills and expertise. K-Station operated on Domino platform. Therefore, it was not beneficial for companies who had Windows platform as they incurred heavy costs in the form of training and conversion from Windows NT to Domino[20] platform.

The competitors of Lotus K-Station were Microsoft SharePoint Portal Server 2001, Viador E-Portal, and PlumTree Corporate Portal 4. These products operated on Windows NT or 2000. With respect to the creation and layout of content, the K-station was considered the best product among its competitors. The portals were designed and organized and the approach used was simpler and more pleasant to use. The K-station enabled the users to create a project-specific virtual workplace where roles and accessibility of the members were defined.

The search agents of knowledge discovery server were simpler. The user interface was easy to navigate through drop-down menus and tabbed pages. Even with all these user-friendly features, PC magazine concluded that it was a "most restrictive product." As this product had the tools to make information visible, privacy[21] and trust issues[22] were of concern in 2002-03. IBM modified this product again to improve the user-profiling abilities. However, it was not very successful and finally, in 2004, IBM discontinued the sales of Lotus Discovery server products. The Lotus Discovery System was abandoned finally in 2004 and the discovery portal was modified and integrated with Enterprise Information Portal.

IBM Enterprise Information Portal

IBM launched Enterprise Information Portal version 7 in 1999,[23] to access the different data sources and knowledge repository.[24] Data sources included structured data (e.g., databases, Lotus Notes[25]), unstructured data (e.g., e-mails, files) and data from specific process or enterprise applications (ERP, CRM, etc.). Enterprise Information Portals (EIP) was a search engine that brought information from the Internet as well as in-house data. The aim was to offer a single, uniform point through which all enterprise's data sources could be accessed. It provided access to content and had the ability to manipulate these contents through rich set of component and services. Portals helped to reduce the operational expenses that generally incurred when accessing information. This portal personalized data queries, searched highly specific tasks and utilized results from both IBM and non-IBM data sources.

IBM's Enterprise Portal was sold as a single product or was complemented with Lotus Discovery System. This portal was customized to enhance the features to meet client requirements. In 2004, IBM released Websphere Portal version 5.0, an updated version of Enterprise Information Portal. The administration capabilities, collaborative capabilities and configurability options were improved in this version.

With respect to IBM's competitors, it was observed by *Eweek*[26] that BEA's Weblogic Portal[27] had the best environments for creating portlets and web applications. Plumtree Corporate Portal had a very high level of customization and design flexibility. It also had the complete search, supported Java and .NET and the application administration was well-suited for enterprise-scale deployments. In 2003, a leading IT magazine, *Dataquest,* rated this Portal to be the best as it was well suited to help customer start web applications at a lower cost. Vignette's Application portal offered the best and most detailed portal administration interface. Finally, in 2004, Websphere Portal 5.0 was rated leader in EIP by *Eweek.* It was also awarded the excellence awards winner in portals and knowledge management. In 2005, Websphere Portal was rated the most expensive product. (Annexure VIII provides a list of competitor products with pricings.)

The Websphere portal was offered as one of the knowledge management products under the umbrella of On Demand Business. Other products, in On Demand Business included Lotus Process and Document management, and On Demand Workplace. On Demand Workplace was similar to Lotus Discovery but was more sophisticated and user friendly.

On Demand Workplace

In 2003, On Demand Workplace was installed in IBM where employees could share and transfer knowledge across the globe (Annexure IX). This workplace helped employees to search for the profile of other IBM employees. It consisted of products and technologies that could connect people, business process, reveal and store information. By 2005, On Demand Workplace had 15 products and came under the umbrella of On Demand Business.

IBM integrated all the contents of its different websites into On Demand Workplace. The statistics showed that 81 percent of IBM employees could access the On Demand workplace. Employees would save 30 minutes per day of their time by quickly locating information relevant to them. Since 2003, On Demand Workplace helped IBM to save more than US$680 million.

This workplace featured role-based portlets that eliminated the need for people to go to multiple places for relevant information. It had manager resource portlets, learning@IBM portlet and blue Pages Portlet. The Manager Resources Portlet, the first global role-based portlet, was launched in 2004. This portlet provided a consolidated view of corporate, geography-specific and local manager resources and HR policy information. Learning@IBM consisted of a detailed profile of each employee with a detailed description on roles of each employee and their area of interest. IBM's Blue Pages was a corporate directory that provided a comprehensive view of the skills and expertise of employees across IBM.

On Demand Workplace enabled people to quickly identify, contact and engage those experts whose skills were required. It also recognized and rewarded collaborative and innovative behaviors, used change management behavior, and reshaped its compensation strategy to weigh business units and IBM performance equally. After the success of this workplace, it was rented out to its clients who needed a collaborative, communication and sharing tools.

Future Outlook

The success of On Demand Workplace prompted IBM to offer it as a product. However, there were many issues that needed to be addressed by IBM like adaptability, pricing and, compatibility.

The pricing strategy was based on the need and requirement of the company. Even if the On Demand Workplace was not expensive, the cost to install and maintain it was high. The pricing strategy was not clear to the customers with respect to the actual cost of the product, and cost of installing with the current system.

> Small companies worry about ease of use, total cost of ownership, and whether they have the skills to manage a new software product. The Express software costs may be low but the service people (to install and maintain it) will kill you. You can't just price Something and expect it to sell. It's your total cost of ownership that matters.
>
> – Tibco chief marketing officer George Ahn, a former IBM employee. [28]

Also, as IBM products were generally not compatible with other platforms, any upgradation resulted in buying expensive IBM products. The compatibility issue restricted the cheaper enhancement that could be done using other company product. IBM competitors warned small and medium sized businesses about the frequent upgradation and enhancement that would be needed for workplace.

> Small and medium-sized business purchasers of IBM products will learn that IBM tends to recommend its own specialized products over less-expensive alternatives.
>
> – John Kiger, Director of Product Marketing, BEA Systems. [29]

Since implementation of this Workplace would result in IBM controlling the technological aspect of the organization, it contemplated whether it would be accepted in an organization. The implementation of Workplace resulted in IBM taking control of the collaborative and communication tools and the portlets of the clients. This made the companies cautious and hesitant to adapt to On Demand Workplace. Consequently, companies were reluctant to sign 10-year commitment with IBM. IBM also needed to educate its clients about the On Demand Workplace so that the functionality of the system was clear to the client. It remained to be seen how this solution would fare in the market and whether it would be successful.

"This utility computing model is bull. Hardly anybody is buying that way. People who were around in the 1970s and 1980s remember what it was like to be owned by IBM. Nobody wants to go back to that."

– Joseph Tucci, chief executive of EMC, IBM's rival. [30]

(T R Venkatesh, Director, Jayaprada MP, Faculty Member and Minita Sinha, Faculty Associate at IBS Bangalore.)

Endnotes

1 Huang, T, "Capitalizing on intellectual capital," *IBM Systems Journal*, Vol 37, Issue 4, 1998.

2 It was a system that had the ability to organize and locate relevant content and expertise required to address specific business tasks and projects.

3 The transformation of key business processes using Internet technologies.

4 Technological development on a nanometer scale, usually 0.1 to 100 nm. One nanometer equaled one thousandth of a micrometer or one millionth of a millimeter.

5 Grid computing was a model for allowing companies to use a large number of computing resources on demand, no matter where they were located.

6 Appointment made by IBM's CEO for people who are well established in their area of research.

7 Awards were given to the individuals who made outstanding contribution and did outstanding research.

8 Awards were given to individuals who made contribution to the computing industry.

9 An honor granted by the President of the United States for inventions and innovations that made significant contributions to the development of new and important technology.

10 An honor given by the President of the United States to individuals who made important contributions to the advancement of knowledge in the fields of behavioral, social and pure sciences.

11 Consulting firm.

12 www.ibm.com.

13 WebSphere Information Integrator software gave real-time, integrated access to structured and unstructured information across and beyond the enterprise.

14 A prestigious industry award.

15 Also known as content management.

16 The ICM AssetWeb provided organizational support centering around competencies, asset management support, and structured collaboration support.

17 Portal was a gateway, for a World Wide Web site that was a major starting site for users when they got connected to the Web or that users tended to visit as an anchor site.

18 Storage space assigned to store data in different forms.

19 Microsoft Internet Information Service.

20 A subsidiary of IBM.

21 Information about relationships among people and entities was made visible.

22 Trust was important to enhance the relationship among employees.

23 www.ibm.com

24 Information that was stored in databases in the text, number or pictoral forms.

25 A product of IBM where viewpoints could be exchanged.

26 Magazine about information technology news, hardware, security, networking, software product reviews and testing, case studies, and research.

27 Enterprise information portal under the banner of BEA.

28 "Integration Vendors Speak On IBM's Mid-Market Push", Informationweek http://www.xmlmania.com/news_article_16-Integration-Vendors-Speak-On-IBM-s-Mid-Market-Push.php, 2003.

29 "Integration Vendors Speak On IBM's Mid-Market Push", Informationweek http://www.xmlmania.com/news_article_16-Integration-Vendors-Speak-On-IBM-s-Mid-Market-Push.php, 2003.

30 "IBM Growth Engine Sputters," http://www.forbes.com/technology/2005/02/24/cz_dl_ibm.html, March 2005.

31 www.research.ibm.com

32 Search of large stores of data to identify some sort of pattern.

33 Search of large stores of data to identify some sort of pattern.

34 http://www.research.ibm.com/km/

35 Transfer of tacit knowledge from one individual to another. Tacit knowledge was knowledge possessed by individuals. Explicit knowledge was knowledge that was coded in computer program.

36 http://www.research.ibm.com/knowsoc/project_summary.html

37 In terms of new business, products and markets that are created.

Bibliography

1. Dragan, R. V, "Lotus K-Station 1.0 Portal." *PC Magazine,* 2001.

2. Gongla, P; Rituzzo, C.R, "Evolving communities of practice: IBM Global Services experience" *IBM Systems Journal,* Vol 40, Issue 4, 2001.

3. Goyal, A. "The On Demand Workplace: Changing the way People Work." *E-Business Review* 1-9, 2003.

4. Harney, J. "Delivering on the promise of enterprise portals-Part 1." *KM World* 14(2): 10-13, Feb 2005.

5. Huang, T. "Capitalizing on intellectual capital." *IBM Systems Journal,* Vol 37, Issue 4, 1998. IBM."IBM WebSphere Information Integrator Portfolio Overview: Integrating Data and Content On Demand." CIO, 2005.
6. KnowledgeStorm "IBM Knowledge Management Solutions and Research." *KnowledgeStorm* 2005.
7. Lesser , E and J. Storck "Communities of Practice and organizational performance", *IBM Systems Journal,* Vol 40. Issue 4, 2001.
8. Lotus, D. C "Knowledge Management Products." *White Paper:* 1-18, 2001.
9. Lyons, D. "IBM's Growth Engine Sputters." *Forbes,* 2005.
10. Pohs, W; Pinder, G; Dougherty, C; White, M. "The Lotus Knowledge Discovery System: Tools and Experiences", *IBM Systems Journal,* Vol 40 Issue: 4, 2001.
11. Rapoza, J. "EIPs more compelling than ever." *Eweek (Enterprise news and reviews),* July, 2003.
12. Rapoza, J. "Portals and knowledge Management." *Eweek (Enterprise news and reviews),* April 5, 2004.
13. Schirmer, A.L, "Privacy and knowledge Management: Challenges in the design of the Lotus Discovery Server" *IBM Systems Journal,* Vol 42, Issue: 3, 2003.
14. The Delphi Group, I., Boston. Knowledge Management Update. *Computerworld,* 1998.

Websites

1. www.ibm.com
2. http://www.daytonitalliance.org/KM-GDITA/gdita-kmcop-kmoverview.asp
3. www.informatica.com/solutions/resource_center/glossary/default.htm
4. http://en.wikipedia.org/wiki/IBM
5. http://www.funderstanding.com/communities_of_practice.cfm
6. http://www.forbes.com/technology/infrastructure/2005/02/24/cz_dl_ibm.html
7. http://www.kmworld.com/news/
8 http://lotus.com/products
9. http://www.computerworld.com/news/2000

Annexure I: Overview of Knowledge Management

Knowledge management has been defined as a method to simplify and improve the process of sharing, capturing, organizing and storing different forms of knowledge. There were two aspects of knowledge management. One aspect dealt with the knowledge possessed by individuals in the form of experiences, insights and skills derived from education and training. This formed the tacit aspect of knowledge. The transfer, capture and sharing of tacit knowledge generally took place through socialization or through communication and collaborative technologies like e-mails, telephones and other communicating technology. The other aspect of knowledge management dealt with business processes, rules, reports, databases and policy manuals. This formed the explicit aspect of knowledge. Capturing business processes and reports brought many aspects of business into focus that previously existed in isolation.

The objective of any KM initiative was to capture the valuable experience and knowledge of an employee. The experience that old employees have over a project like failure or success of a particular approach, and lessons learned during implementation were all captured using technology and stored in data repository. This helped new employees to get information and to understand how to handle similar projects thus reducing the learning and training time. Knowledge management initiatives enabled employees to make better and informed decisions within a shorter time. A survey conducted by The Delphi Group, Inc., in Boston with a group of executive showed that knowledge management was important for the business. It was believed that knowledge management helped to facilitate and accelerate learning among employees. Knowledge management was important as it helped an organization achieve competitive advantage and improves organizational performance.

For a knowledge management initiative to succeed in an organization, it should address three major components: People, Process and Technology. The people of the organization should be such that they adapt to changes that would occur when implementing knowledge management initiative. To implement any knowledge management initiatives, a re-engineering of business process was required. The re-engineering of the processes should be such that it does not change the way business is done drastically. Information technology played an important role in any knowledge management initiatives. The organization should possess communication and collaborative technologies that enabled people to share, communicate and collaborate.

There are four major processes that were used for knowledge sharing and collaboration. These process involved making knowledge visible, increasing the sharing and capturing of knowledge, building knowledge infrastructure and developing a knowledge culture. The culture of an organization played an important role in the acceptance and use of knowledge management initiatives. The culture of the organization should be such that it should promote knowledge sharing and creative activities. Management support also played a crucial role in the acceptance and implementation of knowledge management initiatives. Management support included creation of compensation schemes to motivate employees to use knowledge management systems.

Source: Compiled by ICBR.

Annexure II: Revenues of 2004 from Different Product Segments

Results of Continuing Operations
Revenue

(Dollars in millions)

For the year ended December	2004	2003	Yr to Yr percent Change	Yr to Yr percent Change Constant Currency
Statement of Earnings				
Revenue Presentation:				
Global Services	$46,213	$42,635	8.4%	3.1%
Hardware	31,154	28,239	10.3	6.5
Software	15,094	14,311	5.5	0.6
Global Financing	2,608	2,826	(7.7)	(11.5)
Enterprise Investments/Other	1,224	1,120	9.3	5.2
Total	**$95,293**	**$89,131**	**8.0%**	**3.4%**

Source: www.ibm.com

Annexure III: IBM Research Center

Research Center	Location	Research Area
T. J. Watson Research Center	Established in 1961, this center comprises 4 facilities located in Westchester county, Yorktown, New York and Cambridge. It comprises three sites and four buildings. The main laboratory is located in Yorktown heights. It has roughly around 1793 employees in all the facilities combined.	Computer science, database, data mining, business intelligence, user interface, storage systems software, materials science, nanotechnology, life sciences, services research, mathematics.
Almaden Research Center	Located in San Jose, California, it has about 500 employees.	Computer science, database, user interface, web software, storage systems software & technology, physical sciences, materials science, nanotechnology, life sciences, services research.
Austin Research Laboratory	Established in 1995, this research facility is located in Austin, USA. It has about 74 employees.	High performance/low power VLSI design and tools, system-level power analysis, and new system architectures.
China Research Laboratory	Established in 1995, this research facility is located in Shangdi, in the northwest of Beijing.	Business integration and transformation, information and knowledge management, future embedded systems and devices, resilient and pervasive infrastructure, and user interactions.
IBM Haifa Labs, Israel	Established in 1972, the IBM Haifa Labs include the Research Lab in Haifa (HRL), the Haifa Development Lab (HDL), and the Haifa Software Lab (HSL) in Rehovot. It has around 490 employees.	Storage and business continuity systems, verification technologies, multimedia, active management, information retrieval, programming environments, optimization technologies, and life sciences.

Contd...

Contd...

Research Center	Location	Research Area
IBM Tokoyo labs	Established in 1982, there were 188 employees in Tokoyo labs. It is located in Yamoto, Japan.	Analytics and optimization, software engineering, middleware, system software, security and compliance, electronical and optical packaging technology, engineering and technology services, text mining and speech technology, and accessibility center.
Zurich Research Lab	Established in 1956, this center has 250 employees working in different areas of computer science and systems.	Nanoscience nanotechnology, semiconductor technology, storage systems, advanced server technology, systems design, IT security and privacy, business optimization, mobile enablement, services research, industry solutions lab.
India Research Laboratory	Established in 1998, this facility is located in Delhi. It has around 110 employees.	Speech technologies, pervasive computing, e-governance, information management, knowledge management, e-commerce, life sciences, distributed computing, software engineering.

Source: www.ibm.com

Annexure IV: IBM Research

IBM research started as a small lab on the campus of a major university in 1945. "Think Research" and "Innovation" were the concepts on which IBM Research was established.[31] This part of IBM is totally focused in expanding challenging ideas from their employees, clients academic and government research centers. Their foundation is distributed over many scientific disciplines and they have their own journal in which publications from IBM researchers who explore innovative ideas in different context are accepted for enhancement of knowledge. There were eight research laboratories situated in different parts of the world. Annexure B gives details of these research facilities.

Research in knowledge management (knowledge discovery and data mining)[32] is being done at The China Research Laboratory and India Research Laboratory. As there are a number of unstructured electronic documents and information on the Internet, tools and methodologies are needed to synthesize and organize knowledge as per the requirement of the user. Knowledge Discovery and Data Mining[33] is used to overcome the challenge of extracting knowledge from data. Knowledge Discovery and Data mining[34] is an interdisciplinary area focusing upon methodologies for extracting useful knowledge from data. IBM Research made its mark in detecting and recognizing patterns in a data store in a very high speed. IBM Research gained recognization for machine with learning, text and web mining, and innovative business intelligence application.

The other project which IBM Research was involved was the Knowledge Socialization project that is conducted at T J Watson Research Center. Socialization was the transfer of tacit to tacit knowledge without being captured in an explicit form. Stories were the form of this type of transfer. IBM knowledge socialization project was initiated to identify how storytelling could be included in knowledge management initiatives of IBM. The goal of the project is to identify how storytelling[35] could enhance the knowledge management initiatives in IBM. The other goal of the project was to identify how technology could be best applied to the use of stories.[36]

Source: Compiled by ICBR.

Annexure V: A Snapshot of Knowledge Management Initiative in IBM

Knowledge Management Initiative
1994 Launch of ICM AssetWeb.
1994 Launch of Community of Practice in IBM Global Services.
1999 Launch of Enterprise Information Portal.
2000 Launch of Lotus Discovery System.
2001 Launch of Lotus K-server.
2004 Withdrawal of Lotus Discovery system.
2003 Launch of On Demand Workplace.
Source: Compiled by ICBR.

Annexure VI: Product of IBM for Knowledge Management

Solutions	Technology
DocHouse	Office Information Management system.
eOneCommerce	E-business software.
GEDYS Process Studio	Document Management.
IBM DB2 Content Manager Express Edition	Content Management.
IBM DB2 Information Integrator	Strategic information integration.
IBM DB2 CommonStore For Exchange server	An E-mail Archiving Solution.
IBM DB2 Content Manager for Multiplatforms	Content Management.
IBM DB2 Records Manager	Document Management.
IBM Lotus Process and Document Management	Document Management.
IBM Process Integration Solution Express	Middleware Solutions.
IBM Solutions for Regulatory Compliance	Document Management, E-Mail Archiving.
IBM WebSphere Application Server	Web Server.
IBM WebSphere Business Integration	Business Process Management.
IBM Workplace Services Express	Portals for small and medium business.
IBM Workplace Web Content Management	Content Management.
IBM® WebSphere® Portal	Enterprise Information Portal.
Lecando LCMS -	Learning Content Management System.
up2date	Content Management Server for Small and Medium-sized Businesses.
WebSphere Application Server Express	E-Business Web Sites.

Source: "IBM Knowledge Management Solutions" Knowledge Storm. 2005 and compiled by ICBR.

Annexure VII: Stages of Formation of Community of Practice

	Potential	Building	Engaged	Active	Adaptive
Definition	A community is forming.	The community defines and formalizes its operating principles.	The community executes and improves its processes.	The community understands and demonstrates benefits from KM and the collective work of the community.	The community and its supporting organization(s) are using knowledge for competitive advantage.
Fundamental functions	Connection.	Memory and context creation.	Access and learning.	Collaboration.	Innovation and generation.
People	Individuals find one another and link.	Learn and share experiences, build common vocabulary, create roles and norms, begin a formal history together and establish repertoire of stories.	Trust, loyalty, commitment, tell stories, connect with new members, contribution and participation towards knowledge base.	Problem solving, focused group connection and interaction supports and measures community work.	Change in environment[37] Sponsoring new communities Members enhance knowledge and definition of their field.
Organization support	The organization provides some support to locate and introduce individuals.	The organization recognizes the community.	The organization interacts with the community and learns of its capabilities.	The organization begins to rely on the community's knowledge to contribute to business value.	The organization uses the community to develop new capabilities and to respond and influence markets.

Contd...

Contd...

	Potential	Building	Engaged	Active	Adaptive
Process Support	Identifying and locating potential members Bringing individuals together.	Classifying, storing knowledge, developing ways to support the knowledge life cycle, planning for community operations, beginning deployment.	Socializing new members, managing workflow, executing life cycle process, supporting tacit knowledge exchange, developing and disseminating communications, gathering and managing feedback, correcting problems and adjusting, reexamining and midfying community definition and scope, ensuring self governance and self regulation.	Problem-solving and decision-making. Sensing and assessing the organizational environment. Enhancing community learning and feedback processes. Integrating with organizational processes Linking with other communities.	Focus on innovation. Adapt to environment, exhibit dynamic stability. Develop advance boundary process. Mentor the formation of new communities.
Technology	E-mail, chatrooms, lists, phone calls, teleconferences, on-line forums and directories.	Common repository, initial classification and categorization schema tools, document and library management systems, collaborative work environment.	Portals, expert and community "yellow pages", language translation capabilities, electronic survey, polling and feedback tools.	E-meeting, collaboration toolteam work rooms analytical and decision-making tools. Integration of community technology with the applications and technology of the organization.	Pilot uses of technology. Integration with the technologies. Technology transfer.

Source: Gongla, P; Rituzzo, C.R. "Evolving communities of practice: IBM Global Services experience" IBM Systems Journal, 2001.

Annexure VIII: Price of Leading Portals Products	
Vendor	**Price**
IBM Lotus	• $ 89,000/CPU for Enable • $ 143,000/CPU for Extend
Oracle	• $20,000/CPU for Application Server 10g suite
Plumtree	• $ 75,000/CPU for Plumtree Corporate Portal 5.0 • $225,000/CPU for Plumtree Enterprise Web Suite • $75,000/CPU per component in the Enterprise Web Suite if entire suite not purchased
BEA	• $57,000/CPU for WebLogic Portal, Server and Workshop • $90,000/CPU for those components plus WebLogic Integration
Sun	• $57,000/CPU for Portal Server • $32,000/CPU for Mobile Access • $47,000/CPU for Secure Remote Access • $100/employee/year for Java Enterprise System • $47,000 for Secure Remote Access (require portal server)
Vignette	• $75,000 for Application Portal • $50,000 for Builder • (These are general prices, though Vignette sells according to price tiers depending on factors like number of CPUs users and applications integrated)
Source: John Harney, "Delivering on the promise of enterprise portals-Part 1", KMWorld, Vol 14, 2005.	

Annexure IX: On Demand Workplace

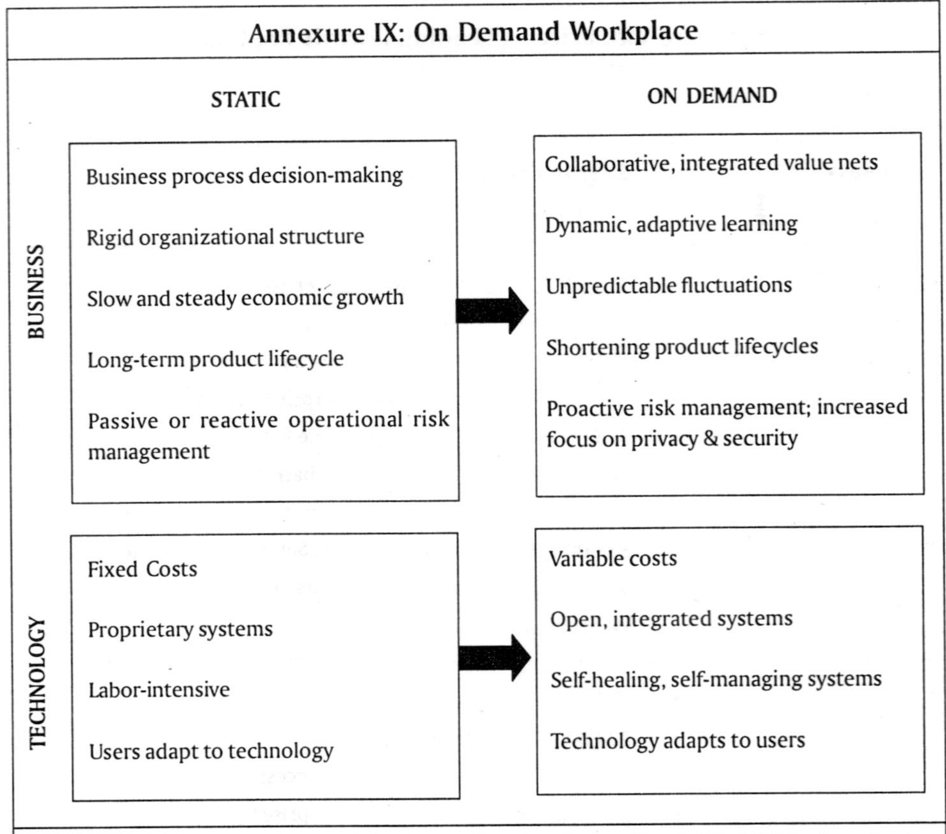

Source: Goyal, A. "The On Demand Workplace: Changing the way People Work." E-business Review (Fall): 1-9, 2003.

Index